Mica-Shards, Moth-Wings

poems of forty years

Mike Shields

in memory of my parents

Hugh Aloysius Shields (1910 - 1977)
Elizabeth Patricia (née) Donohoe (1906 - 1994)

who would like to have seen it

UNIVERSITY OF SALZBURG

SALZBURG - PORTLAND - OXFORD

1996

First published in 1996 by *Salzburg University* in its series
SALZBURG STUDIES IN ENGLISH LITERATURE
POETIC DRAMA & POETIC THEORY
166
Editor: **James Hogg**

ISBN 3-7052-0982-5

INSTITUT FÜR ANGLISTIK UND AMERIKANISTIK
UNIVERSITÄT SALZBURG
A-5020 SALZBURG
AUSTRIA

Distributed in the UK by:
Drake International Services
Market House, Market Place
DEDDINGTON, Oxford OX15 0SF

Distributed in the USA and Canada by:
International Specialized Book Services
5804 Hassalo Street
PORTLAND, Oregon 97213-3644, USA

Typeset in Garamond Antiqua on HP LaserJet 4 by M J Shields, 1996

Cover typography and layout by Warwick Printing Co Ltd on a design by M J Shields

ACKNOWLEDGEMENTS

Some of the poems in this collection have appeared in the following magazines and anthologies:

Alternative (USA), American Poetry Society (USA), Contemporary Review, Dowry, Envoi, Essex Poets, Helix (1972), Here Now, International Poetry (USA), Ipso Facto (Hub), Littack, Mercia Poets 1980, Moorlands Review, Ocarina, ORBIS, Outposts, Pennine Platform, People Within (Thornhill Press), Poema Convidado (USA), Poetry Nottingham, Seam, Stride, Success, Weyfarers.

Contents

Illustrations by Patricia Dennis

Special Acknowledgements

In addition to James Kirkup, one of Britain's greatest 20th-century poets, and my sister, Patricia Dennis, for their contributions to this volume, I must also thank Michael Croshaw for invaluable help and criticism over the years, and Jeannette Vincent, without whose keyboard and computer skills the production of this book and many issues of ORBIS would have been almost impossible. Also my wife Kathleen, my children Richard, Anna, and John-Paul, and all the many friends who have given me support and encouragement over these forty years of poetry.

Foreword: A Man for all Nations

James Kirkup

Speaking as the 'disorganisation man' in person, the multifarious talents of Mike Shields are a source of wonder and envy. I think of him as a series of capital P's -- Professional, Practical, Polymath, Poet. In the contemporary world, such a combination is surely rare. Perhaps because computers are to me an insoluble mystery, the thought of someone being able to write poems on a word-processor, and produce the first-class poetry magazine ORBIS by such means, is nothing short of mind-boggling. Therefore I feel reassured when Mike tells me 'most things computerese are temperamental'. Now I can see the link between the word-processor and that infinitely more subtle machine, the brain of a poet.

The poet who made this book -- in every sense of the *makar*'s making -- tells me that '...the act of getting thoughts and images out and into the area of language is I think the most difficult part of the [creative] process. Certainly my experience as an editor is of seeing again and again poems that are deeply-felt and potentially moving ruined for lack of technique'. The poet's illuminating thoughts on this tricky balancing feat on the tightrope of words provide much of the substance of the introductory essay, the 'poet's credo' that Dr James Hogg ('the Metric Shepherd' in my affectionate terminology) of the courageous University of Salzburg Press asks all his poets to write.

But the really important thing is the poetry, and this Mike gives us in abundance and in great variety. We are both natives of Tyneside, and have both been connected with the Universities of Newcastle and Sheffield, where our poet studied Japanese at a summer course in 1970 as part of his parallel career in technology. I am sure the profusion of themes in his poetry was inspired by his wide-ranging activities and interests, which, apart from editing the literary magazine ORBIS and his current profession as a translator, include music, science, sport, current affairs and politics, food and drink, and bonsai. In Britain, such eclectic tastes are usually looked upon with suspicion, especially when they are transferred to the realm of poetry. The great weight of poets in academe, with their distrust of 'abroad' and of even a working knowledge of foreign languages, militates against those British poets who are looking somewhere beyond provincial academic and domestic themes on the Larkin-Angry-Young-Men model (alas, no longer young, and never all that angry, anyhow!). Mike has always refused to be a 'movement man', and his poetry bears all the marks of European and worldwide cultures that are also reflected in his editing of ORBIS. Will European Union change our hidebound literary outlook? One can always hope. But at least we have in Mike Shields a Man for All Nations, and if ever the bureaucrats in Brussels appoint a Poetry Commissioner, they could find no-one better fitted for the job than the author of this book, who, with a rainbow of languages at his command, can interpret the temperamental unpredictabilities of the passionate computer with the cool linguistic human skills of purely poetic technique, and of purely poetic unpredictability, which is what we call, between art and accident, 'inspiration'.

Mike Shields and I were born just a few miles apart, I at the mouth of the great shipbuilding River Tyne, he further upstream at Jarrow -- the 'Holy City', as the pre-war unemployed used derisively to call it. Though we should not forget that it is indeed holy, for it was here, at *Gyrwy*, that Bede translated the Gospel into Anglo-Saxon, and composed in Latin his great *Ecclesiastical History of the English-Speaking People.* As a child, I often visited his monastery, where I learned legends of viking invaders. Mike also venerates the vikings, as can be seen from the fine poem in *At Somewhat Greater Length* which brings vividly alive the whole of the viking world through the memories of a crippled viking enslaved by Saxons at Jarrow. Another poem, a virtuoso accomplishment of 140 lines in rime royale, *The Ending of King Olaf*, describing the battle of Svold Sound, won the John Masefield Award. Both poems show the poet's love of complex rhyming, tough Germanic rather than smooth Latin vocabulary, and the use of poetic idioms related to skaldic verse. These poems appeal deeply to my own heart and mind, for my family is of Scandinavian origin, and from my paternal grandparents I heard traditional Norse tales long before I was introduced to Grimm, Andersen and Perrault. They have a strange atmosphere of ghostly valour and superhuman magic that I recognise at once in Mike Shields' work.

As a Tynesider, I also appreciate his use of the local dialect, though in print it always looks rather uncouth. But when I read aloud *The Wind and the Waal*, the curious beauty of its vowels and lilting consonants bring back to me the world of my childhood and youth. The North is often evoked, and lovely Lanercost Priory in Cumbria ('ruins sketched against the clouds') inspires a moving historical meditation on commemorative plaques for the family of the Earls of Carlisle (*Offerings at her Feast*). The comparisons are just, and need to be made in our forgetful times.

The universal spirit expressed in such poems that are not purely local can also be found in more intimate personal poems like *Air Moving*, as in the perfectly balanced lines '...And on a morning of such gently-moving air....upon a fundamental bass' (p 61). This poetry of aerodynamics and acoustics represents another important aspect of Mike's work, the world of science, an engineering of poetry to expand its normal range of themes from lyric landscape and historic elegiacs into contemporary mechanics and mathematical discoveries. Instead of blethering about the divorce between science and culture, C P Snow should have been able to study gorgeously-accomplished lines like those on p 62 '...a voice, magnetic echo...engineer's control of air and of its movement'. Sections of this great poem remind us of yet another facet of Mike's range of interests and accomplishments -- musical knowledge and ability as singer/guitarist, with performances on BBC radio and TV.

Such a wealth of poetic invention and scientific vision, combined with rich linguistic skill and loving attention to the details of verse structure and metre, cannot be covered completely in this brief act of homage. I leave it to readers to make their own discoveries of a work that is a perpetual celebration of life and love, all the more poignant because of the darker undertones, the recurrent note of personal and universal tragedy recorded in, for example, *Last Night.* Then, in *Ancient Stones*, that visual shock, across the fields of poppies and wheat, of the '...hulking mass of Chartres,/ man's pile of ancient stones / placating the gods...', that famous view, which never fails to surprise and to catch the heart with a shock of perception. The past in all its weight and wonder imposing its indifference upon our present indifferent times '...in the *Plaça del San Felip*, you understand:/ the shattered stone where automatic fire / bled yesterday's martyrs' (*Barcelona 1985*) Occasional poems? Yes, but what world-shaking occasions they so quietly, patiently remind us of! The deceptive simplicity conceals eternal truths and age-old depths.

Andorra, May 31, 1996

Poems of Forty Years

Mike Shields

Over the years in which I have been editing and reviewing poetry, I estimate I have seen (not 'read', and *certainly* not 'absorbed') between quarter and half a million poems. This apparently staggering claim is quite easily justified in terms of daily post, competition entries, contents of collections, and so on, totalled up over time, and is probably the norm among poetry editors. It may explain why many editors do not publish much of their own work, for it certainly has a stultifying effect in itself, and it also tends to engender a feeling of pointlessness: 'why', one asks oneself, 'add to this already insurmountable pile?'

The answer, if there is one, lies somewhere in parallel with the answer to the question 'why write poetry at all?', to which I contributed my milligram of theory in an article published in ORBIS No 67 (Winter 87). There, I hypothesised that attracting attention to oneself is a major and possibly the fundamental driving force behind all artistic endeavour: 'Most people who write poetry or compose music or indeed create anything at all have done so since childhood', I wrote, adding that perhaps we must have been the sort of children who are always saying 'Look at *me*!, Listen to *me*!'.

Whether I really was such an awful child I cannot say; what I can say is that I do not recall a time when I did not write poetry. The sub-title of this collection, *Poems of Forty Years*, covers only those I am prepared to see published. I have in fact been writing something resembling poetry for well over half a century, now, though what little of the very earliest material has been preserved will remain in its well-deserved obscurity. Whether those poems I have decided to publish should have remained with it I leave others to judge.

This Introduction will, I hope, provide some guidance in that judgement. If there is one thing that has struck me about the many poems and collections of poems that have passed before me, it is how often I have felt the need of just that sort of guidance -- a sort of personal Rosetta Stone to help unravel the often labyrinthine processes that give rise to poetry. Many would argue that poems should be capable of standing on their own merits, and so they should. But I see no reason why the poet should not help readers in whatever way possible: there is no merit in being obscure for the sake of it. It was for this reason that I initiated the *Poet in Profile* series in ORBIS, one of which provided the article referred to above (and one of the very few occasions when I used my magazine to publish my own poetry). So for this reason I am especially grateful to James Hogg not only for his invaluable assistance in publishing this collection of my work, but also for insisting that all his poets should introduce their collections by reiterating their personal 'poet's credo'.

My apparent precocity as a poet is not as significant as it may seem. At first, poetry really *was* just a device for attracting attention, -- something I could do that adults praised, something played like a sort of game at which one won prizes. Likewise, my interest in the classical poetry I was taught at school did not amount to more than a superficial interest in the 'story' element (*Young Lochinvar*, or the *Ancient Mariner*), or on the use of poems as memory tests (I used to amuse myself by memorising long poems in short periods and astonishing teachers). As a result, everything I wrote during those early years was completely derivative and totally unmemorable. Perhaps it is for this reason that I find myself out of sympathy with any concept of 'children's poetry': most children write what is expected of them, and it is only when something jogs them out of this routine that they may actually produce poems of their own and become poets rather than playback machines.

For me, the necessary culture shock came in the form of a fortunate combination of an inspired teacher and an adventurous change in examination syllabus. The first was Dr Vincent Curran, to whom I owe a lifelong debt, and the second a volume entitled *Contemporary Verse*, introduced into the English course for the first time in 1955. Suddenly, I realised that poetry could be vital, interesting, challenging, relevant, and entirely different from the pretty but (to me then) not especially gripping poetry I had encountered. Poets like Day-Lewis, Lawrence, Owen, Spender, and especially Yeats, fired my imagination and showed me poetry I had never experienced before. And I just *had* to write like they did!

Once again the results were derivative: I had exchanged one set of models for another. But I was also learning about rhythm and rhyme, experimenting with blank and free verse, 'unpoetic' language, rhyme-schemes, wordplay, puns, alliteration, and all sorts of less obvious sound effects that I came to see as essential parts of poetry. For if there is one thing that distinguishes poetry from prose, it is the use of 'special' or 'magic' language to heighten the level and broaden the waveband of communication, to describe the indescribable, say the unsayable, bring out secret thoughts and feelings that can be expressed in no other way.

At the time, however, I became frustrated, feeling that I was not accomplishing very much. Also, other things were pressing upon me. Against all advice, I opted to leave school and start work. I had no real idea of what I wanted to do, and was sent to the local youth employment officer, a well-intentioned ex-trade-unionist who had walked the Jarrow March to London in 1936. When I gave writing, music, and languages as my interests, he laughed, telling me there were no jobs for lads there (which is why I tend to snort, nowadays, when women complain about sex-discrimination!). Eventually, I ended up serving an engineering apprenticeship for which I was unfitted in almost every conceivable way, especially in my total lack of mathematical aptitude, resulting in a world record series of failures at university entrance examinations. And, as a weak, artistic, religious boy among rough, hard, mainly godless men, I was faced with another and much ruder culture shock.

The effects of that shock, good and bad, I carry with me to the present day. One good effect was to knock some of the corners off me, rid me of the intellectual snobbery which was one disadvantage of my grammar-school education. I recall meeting one of my workmates in the library, and being surprised to find him there, yet he introduced me to Ray Bradbury and Raymond Chandler, who in their different ways became major influences on my writing. This and other similar experiences taught me that education is not always found in academies and books, though my love of the latter now also extends well over half a century.

Another love in my life has been music. I had shown a similar superficial precocity there too, playing musical instruments in public from the age of about twelve. But the real breakthrough came when by chance I heard a tenor on the radio, and was so absolutely transfixed by the sheer beauty of the sound that, as with poetry, I knew it was something I just *had* to do. For a while, I dreamed of being an opera star, though the true limitations of my voice quickly became apparent. But it was through music that I met my wife, a much better singer than I am, and we had some semi-professional success as a folk-singing duo, appearing on BBC Radio and ITV during the early sixties. Then we married, had children, bought a house, took out a mortgage, and when I next looked up, it seemed, I was thirty.

There was another psychological shock in the sudden feeling that life was rushing away, passing me by. I was assailed by hordes of nostalgic memories, a feeling of age and a longing for the past that would have been amusing in someone so young had it not also been so painful. But it forced me back into writing. I produced my first finished novel, a sheer wallow in nostalgia, and a similarly nostalgic-philosophical poem of about two dozen pages, both of which are, thankfully, unpublished. But they did give me two important insights: first, that writing and especially poetry was going to be the main output for whatever I might have to say, and secondly that the way to write is to *write*. That is not the tautology it might seem to be: what I had discovered was that most of the technical detail, even planning and research, can be left until later. Worrying too much about them at the time gets in the way of writing, and the same applies to poetry. Once on the page, it can be hacked about, but hacking it about before or during writing usually ensures that it will never appear on the page at all.

This new commitment to writing led me to seek out the local poetry group, and to a long-term friendship with its organiser, the poet Tom Kelly. At the time, Tom was editing a small poetry magazine called *Here Now*; because I had some knowledge of print technology, I acted as Associate Editor, and *Here Now* eventually became quite well-known and respected even outside our native North-East. We also published my only collection so far, *Helix*, intending it to be the first of a series of similar booklets. Some of its poems are reproduced in this collection, partly because the exposure they had first time around was, to say the least, slight, but mainly because of their relative importance in pointing the way my poetry was to go.

In 1973, the year after *Helix* was published, I took the momentous decision to move with my family away from the town in which I had been born and lived for the first 35 years of my life to a new job and home in the Midlands. It proved financially disastrous: I was unable to sell my old house in Jarrow, and was left with two mortgages and mounting debts that affected me for years. It was also a time of emotional and spiritual crisis, especially in that the Roman Catholic Church, which had provided me with much emotional and intellectual stability, changed in ways that I could neither agree with nor accept. Again, during the 70s, three friends my own age died, including my best friend, Keith Wilson, who committed suicide, leaving me wondering whether I had failed him, and how. Add to this the normal stresses of a growing family, and it is perhaps unsurprising that I suffered a heart attack at the age of only 37. Then, in the following year, my father died, so there is not much of my thirties that I wish to remember.

There was however one development that had a major effect on my life and poetry: my association with ORBIS and its then editor, Robin Gregory. Robin founded ORBIS in the late 60s, and, after a shaky start, moulded it into one of the major UK magazines, with an additional international dimension it has never lost. I began writing reviews for it while still Associate Editor of *Here Now*, and, after I moved, Robin co-opted me onto the Editorial Board of ORBIS. It did not involve me in very much apart from the reviews I was already writing, but made the initial contact by which I eventually took over the magazine in 1980. Again, I can identify two distinct channels through which the effect worked. The first was exposure to a lot of different poetry magazines, British and American, because of the magazine review column I initiated and wrote for several years. The second was the friendship and support of two other Editorial Board members, Cal Clothier and Frederic Vanson, both now sadly dead, who through their criticism and encouragement helped greatly in establishing what I now regard as my mature poetic style, whatever it is worth.

The poems I wrote during that period, oddly enough, barely reflect the emotional traumata I was experiencing. Perhaps I had already indulged in too much therapeutic poetry, or, more likely, I had by then learned what I am now sure of: that therapy almost always fails as a motor for writing. Whatever the explanation, I began to write poems as a sort of almanac, recording people and places I had known or seen. These fell naturally into a collection which I had a couple of desultory attempts to publish but which never came to anything, although many of the individual poems appeared in magazines. At the time, I had discovered, or rediscovered, three new influences -- Dylan Thomas, Gerard Manley Hopkins, and Walt Whitman -- and it was the third of these who provided me with my title, *All The Slain Soldiers.* But another, and much more important poem was forming itself as the seventies, and my thirties, drew to a close. Coming to terms with my father's death, with the changes in my life, and with the final break from my old home and all it meant, slowly generated *Air Moving*, in some ways the most important poem I have ever written.

It is important not so much in what it expresses, but in the fact that I found my way to express it. For the first time, I felt I was not being moved by influences, that I had no need to experiment with techniques. Like a pianist who has practised finger exercises for long enough, I had become free to express myself without worrying about technicalities. It is not that I abandoned form; on the contrary, I regard myself as a very formal poet. But I feel that I am now able to let the form grow out of the poem as it is being written, and that final shaping can be applied later, if it is needed at all. All the poems I have written since that time have worked in this way, and whatever poetic maturity I am ever likely to reach, I think I reached it with that poem. So perhaps it is time to leave the strictly chronological route I have followed so far, and go through the groups of poems that follow.

Helix

As originally published, this sequence consisted of nine poems plus a brief 'precursor'. Six of the poems are included here, and, though it may seem odd for such a few mainly slight early poems, I intend to spend some time discussing them: the more I say about these, the less I will have to say about those that come later.

Two of the poems justify the 'forty years' in the sub-title: *Snow in the Yard* was written in the winter of 1956, and *Evening, with Cirrus Clouds* in the following summer. Oddly enough, they were both conceived in exactly the same place, the south bank of the River Tyne, at Jarrow, the first on a bitter December morning on my way to work, and the second on a warm summer evening walking home the girl who was later to become my wife. As poems, they both exhibit the effects of the 19th century in my prior poetic education, but also, with their slightly adventurous rhyme schemes, indicate the way my poetry was to progress.

Of the others, *False Spring* and *Delius Summer* are fairly simple records of experiences, the latter arising from my reading of Eric Fenby's extraordinary account of his time with the dying composer Frederic Delius at Grez-sur-Loing. The other two, however, are quite important, and are worth considering separately.

Autumn is remarkable first of all because it was the key poem for this whole sequence, and secondly because it came to me just about fully-formed. In the full fever of my sudden fear of passing time, I was walking through Newcastle on a day that felt like spring but was well into autumn, very near my October birthday, when this poem just appeared in my mind. This doesn't happen to me very often, so I scribbled it down as soon as I arrived at my destination, and it has required very little editing since. It encapsulates exactly how I felt about life at the time, and how I feel about the season of autumn. It is also a conscious tribute to John Keats, and as such makes a valuable point: many people like a particular poem because they identify with it, but the truly great poem is one that convinces against one's total disagreement. Keats' *Ode to Autumn* always did that for me.

Technically, *Autumn* and *Solitary Skier* are also important in that they illustrate something more innovative in the area of rhyme than I had previously been able to achieve. The rhyme-scheme of *Autumn* may seem conventional, but in fact it differs subtly in each stanza; it also features multiple rhyme in places, and, especially, my first whole-line rhyme, of which more later. The latter poem, however, is in many ways a deliberate exercise in poetic technology, and was the subject of another article I wrote in ORBIS (No 46, Autumn 82). The core concept of *Helix* arose in my mind after completing *Autumn*: the seasons repeat cyclically, but never return to the same place because time is also linear, so that the path of life fulfils the mathematical definition of a helix -- aptly, in view of the subsequent discovery that the blueprint of life lies in the double helix of DNA. I already had some seasonal poems, but I wanted one that expressed the absolute zero of mid-winter, the point at which time seems to stop and restart, so I began to create a poem in black and white, using a lot of cold/stark/still/frozen words. The first stanza describes a classic frozen scene, and the second introduces movement -- the skier embodies motion in contrast to stillness. The poem then concludes with a rhythmic section based on the double-beat of the *Kalevala* (the Finnish epic on which Longfellow based his *Song of Hiawatha*) in which the initial motion becomes a rush towards spring. However, it is the first two stanzas that are most important: they are closely interlocked by a cluster of external and internal rhymes, including multiples such as *shadowy skier/Cassiopeia*, but they contrast strongly in ease of reading aloud. This is because the first contains about twice as many stop consonants, making it more 'prickly' in relation to the smoother-feeling second. Although this seemed to arise by accident, it was exactly the effect I wanted to create, and I have made conscious use of stop consonants as flow-controls in poetry ever since.

In its tiny way, *Helix* was a commercial success: it sold out and we recovered the £18 it cost us to print in 1972 (equivalent to about £100 today). As a poetry publication, I have it admit its impact was just about nil: it received only one review, from Peter Finch who was then editing *second aeon*, and I can quote it, in total, from memory: 'A progression of verses that went right past me and off into the grey distance'.

All The Slain Soldiers

As previously noted, these poems all come from a period in the 70s in which I seemed to be producing poetic diary notes. Of the poems in the 'People' section, some were based on individuals I knew personally, others on public figures. I note wryly that I am now more or less the age envisaged by my 30-year-old self in *To An Old Maid*, and that while *For Joszef Mindszenty* was in one way a tribute to the Hungarian cardinal, it was also very much about my own growing disillusionment with the Catholic Church. The final poem of that sequence, *Seniority*, also had a double genesis -- the early retirement of my father due to ill-health, and a BBC 'Play for Today' about the difficulties faced by men in adjusting to retirement.

The poems in the second sequence are based around places and incidents, and are largely self-explanatory, although I might admit to a certain ironic satisfaction with *Light from Hiroshima*, my counterblast to the many facile anti-nuke poems and songs of that period. But there are also poems in this section which show further developments in my 'linguistic' approach to poetry. In *Phom Penh and Elsewhere*, I made use of a carefully-judged register of English to suggest the type of language involved without resorting to 'velly solly' caricatures of oriental accents. In direct contrast, I used Northumbrian dialect in *The Wind and The Waal* specifically to show the local's rejection of the invader and his values. The other area of technical interest is my experiment with 'whole-line rhyme', perhaps the best example of which is *Mountain*. I have always been intrigued by the possibilities and challenges of multiple rhyme, and have long admired the skill of 'wordsmiths' like Cole Porter or Oscar Hammerstein, and the way in which they used internal rhymes to clip the lyric precisely to the tune. My first whole-line rhyme occurred almost by accident in *Autumn*, and after that I experimented with it more deliberately and, after a lot of failures, produced this one successful poem. I also tried whole-line-rhyme sonnets, which (never one to resists a pun) I termed 'supersonnets'. The two more or less successful results of those experiments are included here, though overall I feel with some regret that the form is too mannered and unwieldy to be of much use.

The title poem was the last to be written, and pulls the collection together with a view of life slightly different to that of *Helix*. Here I see time stretching backwards, peopled with a myriad former instantaneous selves, sloughed like snakeskins, or left by the wayside like the corpses fallen behind a retreating army. The poem also makes a slightly supercilious nod to 'found poetry', and a more serious one to the diacritical marks introduced by Gerard Manley Hopkins.

At Somewhat Greater Length

Long poems are out of fashion nowadays, and as a poetry editor I can see why. Indeed, I am grateful to Roger Elkin for being brave enough to devote so much precious space to *Air Moving* in his magazine *Envoi*. On the other hand, there are those who would say that nothing less than 1,000 lines can be called a long poem, but I really do think that the days of the true epic are over for ever: its *raison d'être* was associated with the need to memorise long stories for recitation, and that has now been completely obviated with the twin inventions of print and video recording. However, sometimes a poet might feel the need to speak at somewhat greater length than usual, and I am no exception.

The two 'viking' poems represent my considerable interest in that period, the former being an attempt to summarise the viking world through the memories of a wounded, ageing warrior enslaved in the Saxon predecessor of my home town of Jarrow. The second was my first and only attempt at a rhyme royal, written for a competition in the USA, in which it shared first place.

The poems are not remarkable in themselves, and indeed might attract accusations of pastiche. On the other hand, one can hardly try to recreate the mood and atmosphere of a past time without deliberate use of some archaic language or style, which is not necessarily pastiche as such. And there are some original aspects: in *The Ending of King Olaf*, for instance, the classical rhyme royal form has been extended by the use of para-rhyme to link the end of each stanza with the beginning of the next, and the last line of the poem is a direct echo of the first. In *Viking*, the narrative is interspersed with 'songs', intended to represent the verses regularly composed by viking warriors, who were far from being the brain-dead thugs they are often thought to be. The rules of skaldic verse are complex, so that complex rhyme-schemes have had to be used to suggest rather than replicate them. And, again from a linguistic point of view, the narrative section of this poem has been written using a high proportion of Germanic root words, including coinages such as 'versemakery', a direct steal from the Norwegian '*versemakeri*'.

Dreams are a source of poetry, maybe the only one, because all poems arise from the subconscious, the dark side of the mind, and *Navigator* tries to express this. It is difficult to write a poem about poetry, so I have done the next best thing: written a poem about dreams. Most people ride their dreams like passengers, but the poet is the person who has to record them, like a navigator. And the records are so fragmentary, it is like trying to draw charts on materials as friable and as fragile as one can imagine -- the mica-shards and moth-wings of this book's title.

For me, the most important poem in this section is *Air Moving*, for reasons already mentioned. Unlike previous poetry of mine, there was no conscious attempt to use technique for a specific effect, no deliberate manipulation of language, no search for complex rhymes. On the contrary, it was written as it came, in sections, over a period of about three years, and finally assembled like some sort of jigsaw puzzle. It has three sources -- my father's death, my move from a familiar home, and the emotional shocks of my thirties -- and one unifying theme: air, moving in life, still in death. It comes in my life at its mid-point, the fulcrum around which the past tips into the future. And, in ending with the words of its title, it acknowledges the force of the future, the continuity of life.

Following Springtime

There cannot be many middle-aged men who have not, at some time or other, fallen in love with a younger woman. Often, it is entirely one-sided, so that the woman concerned may even be totally unaware of it. If she is, her reaction may be anything from amusement to anger. For the man, it can be painful, but it can also be beautiful, a reminder of what it was like to be young. The poems in this section try to express that combination of pain and beauty.

Their content is simple enough, and the repeated images of the river of time, the gold of youth, and parallel lines leading off to infinity need no explanation. It may however be worth drawing attention to the rhymes between the last word of one line and the first word of the next, which I feel rivets them together, and gives a sense of continuity provided that the rhymes themselves remain subtle. It may also be worth noting that the conclusion to *Girl, Oh Girl*, which had long eluded me, and which provided another link between the poems (also, incidentally the title of this sequence), came to me on a ferry crossing between Ullapool and Stornoway. It was a changeable, springlike day in early June, with daffodils still in full bloom on the harbourside, and I thought idly how it might be possible to follow the springtime northwards, starting in, say, the Algarve in February. But I also realised how such a journey, taken to its conclusion, could only end in polar winter, and I immediately saw the analogy with an ultimately ineffectual yearning after youth. And so, as they say, a sequence of poems was born.

Places of Work

For some time the only record of the years of my engineering apprenticeship was the first poem of this collection, *Snow in the Yard*. Then, in the late 80s, I began (slowly as is my wont: editing presses on time as well as inspiration!) to produce a series of poems based on those formative experiences. Several are not yet complete (some are still only ideas!), but those that were seemed worth an airing.

Again, they mainly record incidents, but I hope they develop into more than simple diary notes. In almost every case, for example, they were much longer in their initial forms, but have become much more effective, I feel, for being concentrated into fewer words. Also, for reasons which I myself do not fully understand, they have often worked out in two voices. Sometimes this is fairly obviously a contrast between the stronger dialect of the adult workmen and the more prissy English of the artistic apprentice, but in other cases it is less clear. I have theorised that this approach might have something to do with the dichotomy between me-then and me-now (from the 'Slain Soldiers' viewpoint), but that doesn't hold a lot of water, either. I shall be interested in any reactions from readers or reviewers.

In many cases, also, they rhyme -- quite regularly, but in odd and not very obvious ways. For example, *Jack: Accident Report* is a very strictly rhymed poem, but only in the phonological nature of the final consonant of each line: all the 'narrative' lines end in palatal stops (g/k) and all the lines from the 'accident report' in alveolars (d/t). This was not a conscious decision that I took before writing the poem: they were there to be discovered in the initial drafts and simply brought out and edited slightly as part of the polishing process. Since I did not set out with them on my agenda, I am not at all clear as to what function they serve. But once again, they are stop consonants, and they switch off each line, even through enjambments, increasing dramatic punch and poetic tension.

Late Travels

Travel was always something I badly wanted, but never managed until relatively late in life, hence the title of this final section. Hence, too, perhaps, the slightly cynical, world-weary tone in some of the poems. Many were conceived while working in France during 1993-94 -- and the knowledge that my (temporary) employer was an armaments firm might give more depth to the wordplay in *Tank Battle*. Two of the poems, *Prague 1970* and *Autumn Smoke*, are from the original set of **All the Slain Soldiers**, but seemed more appropriate here. The former, especially, fell neatly into a little trilogy, the second of which is part of a much longer sequence initiated by two visits to my friend Louis Rodrigues when he lived in Barcelona, and which may yet be completed, muse and magazine permitting. A visit to Scotland during an incredibly lovely first week in May 1986 produced *Warming*, while *Spring, You Bitch* was completed as recently as a month ago, after the briefest of travels, a drive into the Warwickshire countryside. What they have in common, apart from the travel theme, is that I think they represent my 'mature style', if I can call it that, with less self-conscious striving for effect by the deliberate use of 'poetic technology', and more self-confidence in innate technique arrived at after years of experiment and 'finger exercises'. In the end, this means letting the poem shape itself, which is perhaps something better poets than I achieve much earlier, and with less effort.

Summary: A Poet's Credo?

The question mark is well advised, because I don't really know what a poet's credo is, or whether I have one. Certainly this chronology was the only way I could approach it, because I feel that if we poets do have a credo, it is something that changes with time as we develop (and hopefully improve) our skills and awareness with each poem we write. Indeed, life's greatest irony is perhaps that, just when we acquire enough knowledge and experience to be truly wise, it is time to die.

If I have a set of basic beliefs about poetry, they are: (1) a worthy subject does not guarantee a worthy poem: some of the tritest poems arise from the most laudable subjects; (2) for this reason, I reject all subdivisions of poetry: classifications such as women's, workers, children's, homosexual, are artificial -- there is only poetry, good or bad; (3) the 'goodness' of a poem resides in its *language*; it is the one thing all poems have in common, and the one standard by which they can be judged.

And in conclusion? I still think attention-getting is the engine of creativity. Writing this, I am thinking of how readers will react, hoping they will understand, and be in some way moved or changed. As I concluded my ORBIS *Poet in Profile* article, 'Look at *me*! Listen to *me*! Hear, please hear what I have to say before the inexorable helix screws me out of its other end, and shuts me up for ever!'

Nuneaton, Warwickshire, June 1996.

HELIX

I have become aware of the movement of time
each slow transit of the seasons
a turn along the helix of my life

(1956 - 1969)

1 SOLITARY SKIER

Blue sticks of pencil trees
dull glass, sedge-edged lake
no grass, snow-glow white
acoustics strangely dead...

The shadowy skier skis
a slalom, zig-zag strake
in the alum, lime-rime night
Cassiopeia overhead...

Crystal stars and crystal snow
salt-grain frost on fur and face
wind that cuts like diamond-dust
milk-white frozen moon aloft
down the icy, lead-limbed fell
rushes on, alone, alone
silently through Ragnarok.

2 SNOW IN THE YARD

There's snow in the yard, we know
as we rise at six-thirty, in the frostblack dawn;
no point in cursing, no use for us
to hope for aught but a miserable day
as we trail

out in the snow
and the frosty wrath of a day half-born
for the ferry, the train, the workmen's bus
cap gripped in place, face held away
from the gale.

3 FALSE SPRING

February days of mild air
lead us to believe, all unaware
that winter is not dead, lead us to assume
some god has woken up and rid the world of gloom...

Daffodil heralds brassily volunteer
what false spring leads us to expect,
on every branch, pale butterfly leaves appear,
the phallic crocus draws itself erect...

Poor, ignorant, innocent plants, if they could know,
(the blast of Martial winds, the shroud of April snow)
how old Stepmother Nature loves surprise...
and what of us, who think ourselves so wise?

4 EVENING, WITH CIRRUS CLOUDS

Mare's tails in the sunset, tatters in the sky
wind-torn wisps on the evening breeze
salt-wrack scattered from stormy seas
frozen ferns on a faraway frieze
sweeping the pathways of night on high.

Silver and golden, beauty extreme,
flecked with the flowers of night, and free
to trap those stars, and tangle me
in a marvellous mesh of fantasy
and hold me there in a waking dream.

Silent and lonely, high and white,
pinking to purple and growing to grey,
as evening eases the earth from day
their fragile forms are washed away
before the final flood of night.

5 DELIUS SUMMER

Trees dip languorous leaves in the rancid river
in the afternoon of flat heat --
Florida weather,
Calinda weather.

Before him, music moves in chorded curtains,
dampness condenses in his lungs,
alligators glide
among sickly blossoms.

His boat is stagnant in the stream in the green gloom,
dull sunshine presses in upon his headache,
he dreams of Koanga
and oranges.

Thunderheads are piled pillows in the horizon haze;
time is as paralysed as the viscous water.
To move
is to sweat.

Green room, green gloom in the willows' dome;
he is nailed to the clinker hull by the weight of air,
he is bound by sloth and sleep
awaiting the releasing rain.

6 SICK AUTUMN

Today, there was ice in the air
despite the sun,
a brown leaf sawtoothed past
and I knew the worm was in the year,
another one
gone to the moth and the mildew at last.
Where is summer gone?
I asked.

Sick autumn has come again
I know,
season of yellow days and dying
between the weeks of summer rain
and winter snow,
the wild birds flying,
Why is summer gone?
Where did it go?

Where, aye where, are the songs of spring
today?
Autumn's theme is the lonely tune
of heavy goose-wings wandering
south-away
beyond the sick and swollen moon.
Where, aye where, is summer gone
so soon?

Year by year by weary year
I tend to shun
thoughts of dust and mould,
dreaming of far Iberia,
Iskenderun
dreading the coming cold.
Where is summer gone?
Why do I feel so old?

ALL THE SLAIN SOLDIERS

I saw the debris and debris of all the slain
soldiers of the war

Walt Whitman: When Lilacs Last in the Dooryard Bloomed.

(1970 - 1980)

ALL THE SLAIN SOLDIERS
(after Whitman)

I sometimes think of life as being a route
strewn with the bones of the multifarious dead
manifold, in many rows or ranks,
made up of many parts,
having great diversity.

and these remains, this bony path,
are more than merely dust of men
the mortal worm-crunched powder
trailing out behind the travelling soul,
but skeletons of dead things:
ideas, incidents, books, poems,
states, races, politics and politicians,
works and workings, houses, places,
buildings, structures -
the evidence of man.

We live among the instantaneous am
which, transient, falls between the bones before
the neurones' pulse prods consciousness
and only in the narrow bowl of memory
swirled among the atavistic darks
do we perceive existence
gather reference-points enough
to estimate a course,
divine a future.

There is only a past tense.

Therefore, I commemorate the past -
all the slain soldiers of the war of time -
offering a song in thanks
for these genérative deaths,
weeping selfish tears,
chanting *dies irae* for my own salvation;
chanting for us all, who,
drawing on the wealth of their estate
remain upon the road
to travel and to suffer.

Part 1: People and Other Soldiers

THE MAN WHO JOKED WITH DEATH

He was the man who joked with death,
the undertaker; planted thousands in his time
and cheered their mourners with a tactful skill.
His stories were town-famous;
no funeral he ever made was sad for long,
and, in the bar,
dark-jacketed, pin-striped
(working clothes, he claimed)
he broadcast laughter.

One day, the pain
that scratched his back from time to time
changed nails for knives,
forcing him to consultation and conclusion:
'How long?' 'Not long. I'm sorry'.
'Ah, never mind. I've seen it plenty times!'
Then home to tell his wife
sort out the business,
make a coffin to his measure
and, three weeks later, borne
by four unsmiling men
(dark-jacketed, pin-striped)
to his terminal bed.

Some who can believe, as he,
there is another place to which we go
will see him joking with the shades,
amusing angels, jollying heaven.
Maybe so. But at his funeral
jokes were few.

TO AN OLD MAID

You are five years older than I,
and I recall
how my sixteen looked upon your twenty-one.

You were gloss and gleam and curve and fullness of flesh,
you were breast and buttock, ankle and knee,
coil of copper and sheen of silk.

There were around you in their number
men to my youth -
firm muscles, dark voices, confidence -

and I would have given all my worthless life
if I could have fluttered away its force
in just one, ecstatic joining with you.

You were utterly proof against my callow lust.
Glass-walled behind my anonymity, my fear,
I watched at the edge of the adulous crowd.

You did not know me then;
you do not know me now,
though I know you.

I have watched while my desire faded with your beauty,
and have seen you turn them all away, engrossed
in the mirror-image of your own perfection.

I have seen your struggle with clothes and hats and paint,
your hair-colour changing with the seasons
that marked the advancement of your years.

I watch you now at sixty,
still slim, your fullness unfulfilled,
your door forever shut against the thrust of man,
against the birth of children.

I see you casting bread upon the water,
feeding the swans in wrinkled silence,
reaping no harvest even here.

I move away.
I do not speak.
I never did.

LADYBIRD

Like a sculptor with a marble block
I see, within her outer bulk,
twenty years and many dinners since,
the killer-queen she might have been
once.

Oh, Lady Bird,
you have attained the middle time,
mature, secure, you choose the wine
with confidence,
disarm with marmalade charm
the visitors your boss desires
to influence.

Oh, sad Lady Bird,
sexually extinct,
jealous of your juniors,
sickened when you think
how men who pay you compliments
seek only a director's ear,
chuckling the while behind your
succulent-hammed rear.

Oh, sad, sad Lady Bird,
did it not occur that you
would come to this,
Best Office Girl of 1952?
You store within your queen-bee frame
sugar-acid for your hates;
a grim and futile future waits
for lonely
bitter
Lady Bird.

LUIS ALBERTO

He merited more than a paragraph
this man of Paraguay,
but there it was, parenthetically
inserted at the column foot:

Luis Mesa, also known as
Luis Alberto del Parana
found dead in London hotel room.
Foul play not suspected.

Relegated to late news
it confirmed no note of his music;
for him no N'Orleans Satchmo blues
procession, no adulous crit, no
black-rimmed Times obit.

So I must raise for him a lone verse-voice,
tell how he shone his teeth at us
addressing us in comic polyglot,
and how the harp's bird-carillon
twined among the mesh of multi-rhythmed guitars,
how Julio climbed the high frets
as, with sun-white satin
warming us within our winter hall
Los Paraguaýos entertained.

A swan has died amid brown buildings
and a songbird in among the traffic;
perhaps his passing did not cause the earth to quake
but in my life at least
the light is less.

FOR JOSZEF MINDSZENTY
(1892-1975)

Ah, my old and lost Hungarian Catholic friend
dead today and gone for your reward,
will you, this day in paradise, achieve a martyr's pension-right,
an iron-and-haematite crown to mark your years of war?

Once, a million flights of prayer a day
went for your release, mine among the crowd,
for then you were a prodigy
the Church's rock in Hungary.

But enemies with cogent forces broke you to their way
made you repeat in court the sort of things you thought
you'd never say, hoping via you
to crush a people and their faith.

Nowadays, they do it rather better, never
smashing from outside but rotting from within,
as you have found, old friend, when, just to get you out
and not to cause embarrassment, the Vatican agreed to everything you
asked
then had a 'change of policy' once you'd been pushed aside.
Holy Mother Church will have a lot to do to live that down for me!

The dead make better heroes, comrade Cardinal,
and now they've laid to rest your narrow skull and deep accusing eyes
they may find kinder things to say of you.
No canonisation, mind! No future child be named
for martyr Joszef, Saint of Budapest,
but just a word for you and Slypy and the rest
betrayed like all of us by men unworthy of our trust.

We never met life. I wish we had.
But maybe in a place beyond the grave
we'll meet some time - in paradise, perhaps,
though if, by chance, you find your heaven full
of swinging bishops playing politics
well then, old much-admired Hungarian Catholic friend,
we'll meet in hell!

SENIORITY

It seems like more than half a year
since formally they disposed of me
with food and drink and laughing friends
and, from the management, a gift
ironically to measure time.

At first, it seemed that there was much to do:
the garden, and of course the house,
but, counting every room, there's only eight
to decorate, plus stairs and hall.
I'd do them all, would funds permit,
but, there again -- for whom, for what?

For my wife, of course, and for her pleasure
a major task in choosing tones and patterns
and this or that in carpets that we can't afford.
For her, the same unending tour of stores and markets,
friends for coffee, meetings, social evenings,
in which I never did participate.

Is woman more adaptable?
Has she been trained for this?
Or did her patterns alter long ago
when fluids dried, and when the litter left the nest?
And did all this occur beyond my sight?
And if so, why, and why did I not see?

Those other things I thought I'd do --
write, study, paint: no use, too late,
all that I'd intended to create
must have been indexed, stored, and lost
in cells my brain discarded years ago.

Now, I have the whole slow day in which to contemplate
the torpid turmoil of my brain-snail,
in which to practise stillness,
steel myself against the cold,
learn the tricks of waiting and of silence.

Five dozen years and five I've had
and five perhaps remain;
five years in which I must acquire
the ways of chill and quiet,
five years in which to serve
a full apprenticeship for death.

Part 2: Battles and Old Battlefields

TELEVISION WAR

We died before your eyes at Hué,
flamed from sky to Sinai sand,
in Bangla, rotted by your supper-tray,
posed for our Biafran execution.

We are the immortal soldiers,
anonymous newsreel extras
dying down the aerials of the world.
And you, with eyes
conditioned by a thousand acted deaths,
watch unperturbed across your living room.

Is it because my face is dark
that you so lightly entertain my death?
If this were York (old/new), or Birmingham,
would you then at last accept
my body and my blood?

Oh yes, we know you feel concern,
that you allow your governments
to send us teams of peacemakers,
toothless troops in sky-blue helmets
set between our hates;
when they move in, the camera teams will leave
in search of further colossea.

But, one peak viewing hour, we might change your script,
turn our tanks towards the lights,
sight our mortars on the spying cameras,
brave reporters shirtsleeved now against
machine-guns that are more than soundtrack,
interrupt our war for long enough
to clear away a mutual enemy,
and then at last resume our fight
to die, if not in peace,
at least unwatched.

TERMINAL

Spring Friday at six:
we, standing
damp, impassioned,
in clearing weather.
A bisected sky:
east tarred, bloody,
lit by western footlights.

There had been
some sort or quarrel;
I recall only the relief,
only the fading storm,
only the renewed vision
of a sweet future.

Now, in dying daylight,
that future about us, behind us
still the garbage of old gods
rattles among dark rafters.

We have a terminal condition.

BERSERK

Steel could not touch them
nor man withstand
the berserks
shield-biting, sword-clanking
raging themselves invulnerable.

After noon I understand a truth
denied to me midmorning
among the pains of loss and love,
for now, past all the years and times apart,
at last I love and do not fear,
uncaring for myself, or for my pride.

We berserks are beyond care:
we feel no pain.

ON VIEWING DURHAM CATHEDRAL FROM THE TRAIN

Now the grisly diesel ogre drags me
rattling
through quarried heaps of miners' spoil;
now the bulging, blackstone-buttressed arches
dripping
trip my eye with waxing speed;
now the welded, sleepered, cold-steel pathway
whining
rings to the assault of whirling wheels,

and rows and rows and rows and rows
of slated, brick-built terraces
pour their fume into the innocent air.

Around a curve and, singing, into view
majestic organ notes of architecture stand:
a city crowned with castle and cathedral,
moated by the oxbow-twisted river;
brown stones, wine-tinted by the dying sun,
cloud-soaring, rooted in the Rock,
seen, face-to-face, through half a mile of air.

So, the duality of man's dreams, the old, the new.
The mind loves the machine; the heart, the view.

THE WIND AND THE WAAL

(written in the Tyneside dialect after a visit to the Roman Wall at Housesteads, May 1970)

Aye, Roman, the wind blaas caad agin the Waal,
caad oot the north, where the snaa lives,
where the wolf lives,
where the Pict lives.

Aye, Roman, ye're in the caad lands noo;
nee women in silk wi' wine and oil,
just us, and the wind,
and the Waal.

Aye, Roman, it must be a lonely life,
tribune to troops o' foreign scum, Jarmans and Africans,
the scourin's of the world
guardin' a single city.

Aye, Roman, we knaa, ye've tellt us,
they're barbarians oot there, paintin' thor faces;
we've got civilisation
... but they've got freedom.

Aye, Roman, thon's yor Waal,
slashin' the country's throat across,
built, ye say, to keep them oot
... aye, and us in!

Aye, Roman, it's a canny waal,
but it's not the forst waal in the world,
nor'll it be the last;
waals and cortains,
stone and iron.

Aye, Roman, it's a caad wind the neet,
it'll be caader yet come winter;
ye've made a canny waal to keep men tied.
but ye cannot keep the wind oot, Roman,
ye cannot keep the wind oot.

OFFERINGS AT HER FEAST

(Lanercost Priory, Cumberland, 1970)

*'... this empire has been acquired by men who... freely gave
their lives to her as the fairest offerings which they could
present at her feast.'*
Pericles: Funeral Oration: Thucydides, BkII (trs Jowett, 1900)

Out of the hills, we
came into a region pleasantly flat;
a grey, unhurried northern day,
cool and bushy in the middle of the year.
We found the ruins sketched against the clouds;
paused, listened to the stones awhile,
sheltered from a sudden rain,
read the unknown names on graves...

... then found the corner kept for local earls,
reading history in their stones,
noting, too, the plaques recording
deaths remote from these resigned and tranquil walls,
sons and daughters sacrificed in savage lands,
children, dead by bullet or disease,
victims for the gluttonous goddess empire,
offerings at her feast.

Somehow, we must learn to pity them, these nobles;
like the Jew, they bled, and like the poor
their blood and tears were salt.
How easily and callously we assume
that wealth was compensation for a martyred child,
that envied power had no price.
How can we think to have improved, when all we do
is to replace an older arrogance with a new?

SUPERSONNET TO THE POET AT BEDE'S MONASTERY

(on the river Tyne, at Jarrow, built about 650 AD, now partly preserved amid the industrial squalor surrounding it.)

... and when you come upon this church, these stones,
placing your trusty feet on national grass,
you, of all men, should hear the dirge intoned,
as plainsong-brothers meet in Latin Mass,
and you'll ignore the ships, the mire, the tanks,
the ever-present smells of oil and gas,
and know once more the atmosphere of thanks,
the incense-smoke of *deo gratias*;

then comprehend that (though your mind rejects
the incommoding strangeness, psychoclast)
this same millenial-blowing, retrospec-
tive wind comes flowing changeless from the past.
Then you'll be utterly leached of metaphors;
mentally crushed beneath the weight of years.

SUPERSONNET ON SCIENCE-FICTION

(after Keats on Chapman's Homer)

Much have I travelled, overwhelmed by cold,
thrilled with the mine of space, the star-rich seams;
such were my savants: Kuttner, Heinlein, Gold,
filling my nights and days with arcane dreams.
So, I have flown the spacewarp alleyways,
(endless arrays of snailshell clouds of light)
pitying all the lonely suns ablaze,
friendless in layers of everlasting night.

When man goes out, in some transcendent scheme
beyond our death, in pillared powering flare,
he may allow that we could have foreseen
his restlessness. On this account I dare
to feel a certainty that those who do
will read these words, and, by them, know we knew.

MOUNTAIN

Why did we tread the baser tracks
of rock and boulder, fording beck,
the back- and shoulder-mauling trek
by giddy edges, razorbacks?

Why weary nerve and sinew, why,
by crag and rising, narrow ways,
the agonising paraphrase
of dreary urban stimuli?

The questions hang irresolute,
immobile; yet perhaps we find,
in post-climactic, aprés-climb
exhaustion, that we guess the truth.

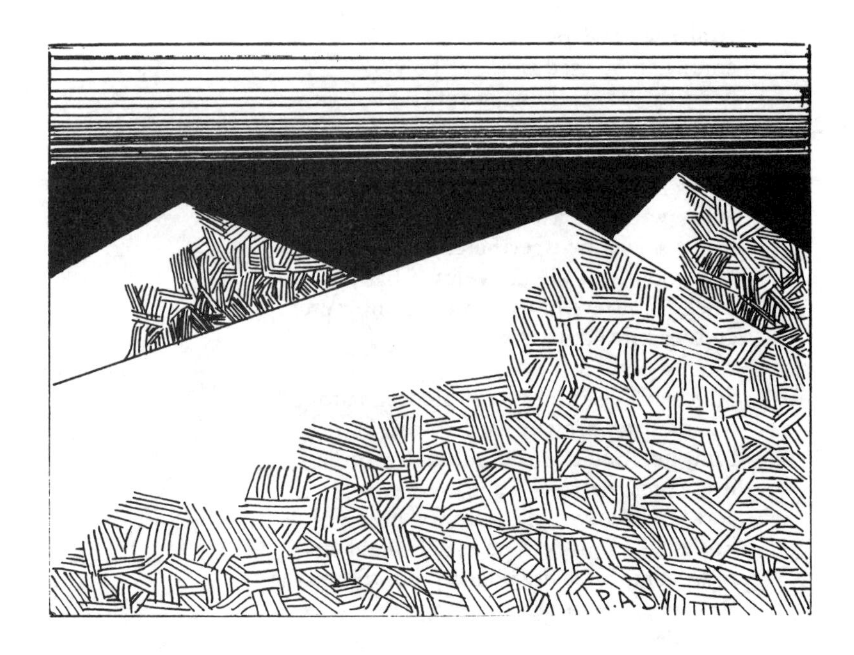

FOREST

(Epping Forest, December 1974)

Unlike my Tapio-haunted, tongue-daunting
pinecushion on the wildmoor,
fir against waste wind,
this English forest drove me to words.

It was mildest December
when I walked its wide, contrasting spaces,
ducked cantilever branches,
scuffed copper-alloy mould
from beeches pillaring the clouds
with castellated chalice of trunks,
large old elm, larch,
arthritic oaks
and pines longing for the light.

And I was aware, too,
among these aged trees, of how
beneath the crackling cover,
deep-rotting roots of ancestors
burrowed to the bedrock,
an archaeology of vegetation,
and saw how ancient primitives
heard spirits whisper here,
saw goblins in the convoluted bark,
smelt monsters in the dwarf-stump outcrops,
and feared the witchwood.

So I faced again my own preoccupation,
felt the past present itself to me,
tying me numb and dumb and wordless
in among the woods and weeds
and leaves leaving largesse for next year's growth,
knowing I must escape that I might make
my poem, for, with silence and with savage age,
this forest swamped the song
it made me sing.

PHNOM PENH AND ELSEWHERE

Your lordship is large and has great wealth
possessing many bright machines by which he lives,
he is finely dressed and strong;
can he notice this low person?

Can he hear this unimportant voice
which asks: it is untrue, of course,
that he will leave us now?

Naturally, we have been unworthy of his strong protection
slow and stupid in the art of war.
It would be just were his councillors deciding
that his greatness now requires that
he go some other place.

Clearly we have proved our foolishness:
our buildings are destroyed, our guns abandoned,
that unfortunate bloodstain there
that was my youngest brother
but he, having been small,
will not be missed
except perhaps by her who brought him life
if she still lives.

It is perhaps a pity we have come to like
the way of life your lordship recommends;
those at our gates would not agree
that we continue in this way
were your lordship to depart.

We do believe he will ensure for us
peace with honour, as he has said before,
and are most humbly glad he stays with us
despite our obvious inability to match his shadow.

Therefore lord, we have convinced ourselves
that what we see emerging from his chimneys
is fume from fires lit to keep his lordship warm
and not portending smoke of burning paper.

GLADIATOR

We are gladiators,
we live among theatres of war
lightly armed against the enemy.

We are gladiators,
we face our fate among the sands
and die, trapped in their flow.

For us there is no victory,
no peace, only respite;
there is a dread reason why we feed,
and why our wounds are dressed.

To us, the tragedy is multiple,
for we have seen the man whose blood
already sinks into the timeless sand
be changed from friend to foe to victim.

Each day, the iron gate of morning
opens into fratricidal war;
each day some die and some survive
to pass the gate again and die tomorrow.

There is no choice, no other way,
no reward but to remain noble.

LIGHT FROM HIROSHIMA

The road that man has travelled is deep-riven with the ruts of war,
wars with other animals, with elements, and with himself;
the spear has pierced more freely than the penis
the pen has come to life much later than the sword
and man has often moved and crawled and wept before the harsh commands
brayed from the black throats and sulphur tongues of guns.

We would have waged our wars world-wide far sooner
had we but the power.
Observe how Englishman and Frenchman grappled round the globe,
fought with the conscripted help of helpless folk of every shade of
red and brown,
how, even earlier, Cheng-Chiss' ranged the wide Eurasian plain
how Romans battered every part of what was then their world,
oh yes, the so-called World War One was not the first world war
but just the first that happened simultaneously!

It was, as well, the first in which we fought in three dimensions;
we moved from area to aerial, added the third axis, altitude,
struggled with laws of lift and drag to storm the stormclouds,
fight like eagle-mounted knights with inconsistent chivalry,
shower death upon the nameless crowds below.

This was indeed a new dimension to our warcraft
great machines transporting whole battalions
over Alexander's lifelong conquests in a span of hours
leaving no path secret for the generals' shocking thrust,
spreading generalised destruction with small movements of the hand
as Europe's shattered countries could attest,
as could the twin and tortured cities of the rising sun
over whose people broke at last a new and dreadful dawn.

Do you suppose that, if those bombs had merely been
a more efficient way of blasting buildings flat, of crushing men,
they would have stopped at Nagasaki?
Apart from numbers, what's the odds between, say Hannover and Hiroshima?
Why did not Hamburg, even Dresden, halt the western war?

Perhaps we ought to praise the Bomb, and pass the Lord
our thanks; perhaps the only way we could be stopped
was through our fear - something bigger cowing us,
driving us like dogs before a fire.

The light from Hiroshima glares across the years
laying bare the options with a grey, actinic flare;
by this grim lamp we have at last defined at least
an upper limit to the scale of war
and for the first time in the world
the warlords pause.

SCATTERLING

(Nuneaton Railway Station, Warwickshire, June 1973)

Why shudder as I step off the train?
Sun, flickers warm through sycamores,
strange sustenance for this passage-bird,
this cold cuckoo, this vagrant.

I am no emigré, forced to leave my home,
driven by some cruel eviction to unwilling flight;
I come because I wished it, come for better times,
so why withdraw my foot, why hesitate?

I shall assimilate their different ways:
I am gregarious. And, in any case,
in such a technical and travel-intensive age,
no home is ever far away.

Yet, on this fine and most impending day,
I feel unreasoned squirmings of the gut
at thought of bones unresting in extraneous earth,
of alien children laying flowers on a grave.

AT SOMEWHAT GREATER LENGTH

(1968 - 1980)

VIKING

I was not made
to scrabble earth
by a stinking marsh;
I did not live
that rabble serfs
might name me thrall.
I am free-born
of such a world-
encircling kind
as warlords dread,
and lower folk
obey.

In Trondelag, where I was young,
the pale, wild days of northern Spring
brought birch-white girls from Winter barn
to earthy, cow-untended struggle...

...when we wished we took, but
when they wished they gave,
though lying aftertalk
cried for lost innocence.

other skirts we escaped -
other mothers', as we rushed away
to manhood; swords, ships, steel
and wilder, keener, dangerous play.

(Song)

First trip
to sea;
first ship
to sea;
sea-sick
to be;
home back
to quay...

and the staggering strangeness of the heaving land.

Unhappy with our provincial coast,
where only a meal of stringy cowflesh,
the sack of a yokel's midden
or a poke at some fishcatcher's slut
meagrely rewarded conquest,
we vikked among more distant parts.

(Song)

Fire follows reivers' band
in Viken, More, Halgoland,
hewing Swede and Dane and Finn;
fall of water, canvas rattle,
hauling men of war to battle
vik to vik the longships skim.

Near Lindesnes, Arne died,
in Skaane, Eymund.
Toralf and Torbjorn, brothers,
avenged each other tenfold
when they fell against the Swedes.
Digre Orm, the Fat,
was split by Jyttlanders
returned to the ship
holding himself together
to spill his heavy gut upon the deck
and die at sea.
Our Sea-King, Harald,
six times wounded led us home,
but died of the cough that Winter
like a woman, in straw.

Homecoming, feasting:
glutted and rutted and sotted the whole dark season,
while Aake-Lame set looted gems
in shield and swordgrip,
Gunna wove sails.
Blue-Smith fashioned helms
and Eyvind carved dragons
for storm-scarred ships
awaiting Baldur's Spring
to be reborn.

New-pitched from moorings, red
wind-wings spread,
the vikings head
out along the sea-roads to further wars.

(Song)

The Eastern Sea
bore our ravaging ships.
Öland, Bornholm
wore our scars.
Vindland, Estland
saw our fury,

and we wintered away in their long harbours.

Down the wide, flat, mirror-snake rivers of the marshy plains,
we met small yellow men
who lived on
fought on
were married to
horses.
They shot arrows from a coward's range
and killed many
until we found them in their camp at night
and slaughtered them, and their wives .....

.... and feasted well on horseflesh!

We wintered again in Gardarike,
barely tholed by Northern rulers
who still spoke our tongue
though soiled with foreign gobble
and in the third year turned homeward
richer in gold
poorer in men and ships
not wishing to seek, further south
the land of the Blue Men.

(Song)

Homing sea-wolves run for Nidaros,
thirst for sight of Trondhjemfjord,
knifing water, braving storm....

(the song dies)

... two vessels, forty-two men
returned, hungry, haggard
to places where they had no place
where lads were fathers, girls fat wives
and old men dead
where homes had been outgrown
where time had made us outlanders.

With the wakening sun, we were glad to be gone
tired of warm darkness
sick with fat feeding
bored with talk and song
soft with idleness
sated with tedious women.
We had become fatherless children of the sea
cousins to the lonely shark and the seal
hard with the burning of wind and battle
driven, as are the gods
by the storms of luck and weather.

(Song)

Norn-drawn
faring;
storm-borne
steering;
horn-crown
wearing;
war-torn
forlorn
sea-fowl, we

... landing only to mate and kill.

Yet, westering-over-sea
out of the Tronders' glad farewell,
along the line neither northing nor southing
as the sunboards tell,
we came upon an icy, empty land
standing like a wall out of the *haf,*
against whose basalt foot
mast-high waves broke powerlessly;

but, rounding this bitter coast,
we found long calm fjords
into which clean valleys ran,
where folk made welcome
giving us land and wives
with the kindlihood of those who lose nothing in the giving.

Eight years I was an Icelander,
farming the peaceful valley sides,
fishing the plentiful fjord,
spending my winter days
in versemakery and childgetting,
laying in stores of fat...

... until, one pale morning,
remembering the silver girls of Trondelag,
I saw again the strange light
of the grey salt wastes,
and heard a tern screech...

... and, leaving my farm,
leaving my wife and my young sons,
leaving the hills and the fish, the verse and the songs,
leaving the beasts and the crops and the boat, and all the wasted
years under glass-tipped mountains
I sought ship for Norway.

In Romsdal, I met a lively crew,
eager for the *vikking* sport;
glad, too, of an older hand
upon their steering oar
after their skulls had proved its strength.

We sailed,
untouching Norway, or Denmark,
or the Eastern lands,
for there lived kings whose force
banned the dragon pirate...

... new ways for a changed world.

The Frisian coast gave no reward
-- windy, waste-marsh dunes;
other parts were well-prepared
-- Northman's-Land exiles drove us out.
The decks were hard and wet,
the Spring waves cold,
hunger dissolved the fat of years,
swords hung, bloodless, rusted,
eyes hollowed beneath horned helm...

and so,
treading the path of the westering gull,
we made our ship to this soft land,
where we rove the coast from south to north
until we reached this river,
this town, this fen, this god-lost *Gyrwy*
in which I am entombed.

The remembering takes little time
the twenty crippled years
that I have lived a slave ...

... my leg was broken by a stone
and so I lay abandoned on a spit of land
watching my ship returning to the sea...

... the village folk returned at last
picking through their rubbled homes
shrieking over me like birds ...

... their priests prevailed upon them,
making them spare my life
with the sickening cruelty of charity ...

... they splinted my leg, badly
(I was struggling to reach my fallen sword)
and it gnaws me now, each day.

Gyrwy: Saxon name for Jarrow, meaning 'marshland'

Like a stallion, they have put me to work,
making use of my captured strength.
Like a stallion, too, their women use me -
a child a year to salt their thinning blood.
And, like a stallion, they trust me, warily,
hoping perhaps that the priests
placating their weak god within the blackened stones above me
have gained purchase on my soul
with tasteless bread and watered wine.

So, now again I have a sword;
they wish me to lead them in the next attack,
though some fear that I shall turn
and fight against them with my fellow Northmen ...

(Song)

A fool will fail
the finest school,
and who'll excel
a Saxon fool
that never kenned
nor cannot guess
that Norseman's end
is onefulness.

Maybe tonight the ships will come,
the berserk strangers leap ashore,
and I shall smile because I know
that I will never stand three breaths
against their wolvish rage.

I see the axe cleave wooden shield,
sword split me to the rib ...

... but no straw will lie beneath my coughing corpse,
no woman see me in my weakness,
no priest sicken me with Christ-gabble.

Chance is we have lived too long, we Northern kind:
there is a hexery on the earth
- men herd in houses
huddling the land in lifelong indenture,
Christ-Baldur lives
while Tyr and Odinn sicken,
while Sleipnir stumbles,
the aged Aesir drowse,
the world-steam wilts

... and we, who overlive our time,
make at our ending a wild and deathly song.

(Song)

Who would not welcome death
when life is past?
Its pain is seldom less
than sword-blade's thrust.
How else shall thralldom pass
unless we first
leave this unwholesome path
at any cost?

You from-time folk, you ghosts
of come-to-pass,
for your own sakes, at least
remember us.

THE ENDING OF KING OLAF

'Hvor bliver Ormen Lange?
Komme ikke Olav Trygvason?'

Bjornstjerne Bjornson

Queen Thyre weeps, laments her missing land,
for she'd been Denmark's daughter, Vendland's queen
before she fled to Norway, cap-in-hand
and destitute. Now she forgets how keen
she was to marry Olaf, and, between
her sobs, she calls him coward, foolishly
berates him for her lack of property.

Let's set the record straight: we have to say
King Olaf is a little hard to gauge:
this former viking killer-tearaway
now slaughters pagans in a Christian rage,
sees visions, falls for women twice his age
(thus Thyre's maiden-husband, Earl Styrbjorn
was dead before this king was ever born!).

But coward he is not! He can discern
the danger in a voyage to the south:
he knows now how unwise it was to spurn
Queen Sigrid - even slap her in the mouth
for her insulting words! - and knows that both
her son, the King of Sweden, and King Svend
of Denmark (now her husband) plot his end.

And there is more to this assorted band
than Swedish-Danish cut-throats: now allied
is Erik, son of Haakon-Jarl, whose land
and life were lost when Olaf occupied
the kingdom of his ancestors. Riptide
adventurers may fight for loot or pay,
but exiles battle for their lost Norway.

The King brings Thyre daffodils in May
and salad-herbs, to cheer her nothing loth;
she snatches them and flings them all away,
'*I want my settlements*!'. Then, with an oath
of fateful consequences for them both
he swears, 'You'll have your Christ-damned property
though it be the end of Norway and of me!'.

In Olaf's fights for Christianity,
he'd killed a famous sorcerer, and won
his ship, the *Snake*, the greatest on the sea,
then built one twice as big, never outdone
by any sorcerer beneath the sun!
Now *Snake* and *Long Snake*, gliding silver-oared
precede the King's fleet out of Trondhjemfjord.

The graceful ships float south like drifting birds,
yet, dragon-strong, are ready for a fight.
They pass the Ness, the Narrows, undeterred -
what enemies there are stay out of sight.
The Baltic summer days are long and light,
the winds are kind, the glittering seas are calm:
they reach the Vendland ports without a qualm.

King Boleslas is friendly, and affirms
his match with Thyre's finished (we know why!)
he makes the settlement in generous terms
and Thyre is delighted. Then the sly
Sigvaldi, who in fact is King Svend's spy
sucks up to Olaf, urging him to stay:
his loyal captains chafe at the delay!

It's autumn when at last they put to sea,
Sigvaldi with them. Charming, he insists
he knows a better route: 'Let's you and me
sail close in round the island, while the rest
stand out to northward'. Olaf in his trust
for this smooth villain, lets his fleet divide
and follows in the wake of his false guide.

Around the island lies the Sound of Svold -
the place where Olaf is to meet his fate -
and what they see before them stops them cold:
their enemies' combined fleets lie in wait!
Sigvaldi strikes his sails to separate
his fleet from Olaf's ships, becoming then
the 'scabby dog of Jorundfjord' again.

The King in haste addresses all of them:
'We've been betrayed, lads, now we're on our own,
so lash the ships together, stem to stem
and stern to stern, a trick that has been known
to beat worse odds than this. Though we're alone
against three fleets, they must attack across
our outer gunwales only - that's their loss!

'Remember, too, since Christ, we've come to this
the thousandth year, in which the world will end;
no point in fear, no time for cowardice,
what we must do today is to commend
our names to legend. If God should extend
the world another thousand years, men ought
to marvel, even then, at how we fought.'

The Danes come first - they claim it is their right -
but soon wish they had not: they're beaten back
with heavy losses. Next into the fight
sail Sweden's ships, but their lightweight attack
makes no impression. Then, out of the wrack
come Erik Haakonsson's Norwegians. Here
at last is an attacking force to fear!

The *Iron Beard* is Erik's ship of war
named for the ironclad beak below her bow,
and Erik has not long been there before
he's rammed the planking of each outboard scow,
forcing their men to cut them loose somehow
and then retreat. Ship after ship is lost
until the King's ship stands alone at last.

Young Einar Thambarskelv, on Long-Snake's mast -
the greatest bowman fighting there that day -
sights Erik, sends an arrow hissing past
his head, then feels the great bow *Thamb* give way:
its snap sounds louder than the battle-play!
'What was that fearsome crack?', the King demands.
Says Einar, 'Norway breaking from your hands!'.

From *Long-Snake's* quarterdeck, King Olaf sends
the last few new, sharp swords around his crew,
and for a short while longer, he defends
the remnants of his kingdom, clinging to
the vision that, perhaps, the overdue
main fleet will come to save them from the fate
that otherwise, most surely, must await.

And so they stand together in the fight:
Jostein and Thorkel, Olaf's mother-kin,
his brother Thorkel Nefia, Thorstein-White
his cousin, and Kolbjorn the Marshal, twin
in all appearances to the King, plus, in
the forehold, Berse Bollarsson the Strong -
but even these cannot hold out for long.

Earl Erik now prepares at last to fling
his ropes aboard *Long-Snake* (he wants her whole!),
the Danes and Swedes return, there's everything
to gain now that the Earl is in control,
which means for Olaf's men there's no parole -
by their harsh lights they're dying as men should:
the seat is turning purple with their blood.

The *Long-Snake's* overrun now, fore and mid;
the King's few men cannot hold off the horde,
so Olaf and Kolbjorn, in one last bid
to cheat death and defeat, leap overboard.
Earl Erik lowers boats, offers reward,
but enemy and friend give up their hopes
when it's Kolbjorn they fish up with their ropes.

Some swear that Olaf dived beneath the ships,
survived, went on a pilgrimage to Rome,
but others claim he lies in Svold Sound's deeps
and shoals. However that may be, it's known
he never more returned to Norway's throne.
Olaf goes on to legend's memory-hoard
Queen Thyre weeps, laments her missing lord.

HISTORICAL NOTES

Olaf Tryggvesson (Trygvason): King Olaf I of Norway (995-1000). Descendant of *Harald Fairhair (Haarfagre)*, first king of N., exiled in infancy and brought up in Russia. Spent early years viking; convert to Christianity in England (confirmation sponsor King Ethelred). Reputed killed in battle with combined fleets of Denmark and Sweden, plus Norwegian exiles under *Erik Haakonsson*, at Svold Sound (N Germany).

Erik Haakonson: son of *Earl (Jarl) Haakon*, ruler of Norway, who was murdered by his slave when Olaf T. landed. Erik went into exile in Denmark, which claimed sovereignty over Norway. After Svold, he returned and ruled Norway himself for several years.

Sven(d) Forkbeard: King of Denmark and father of *Canute (Knut Svensson)*. Former ally of Olaf but turned against him when *Olaf* made himself king of Norway; further provoked by his wife Sigrid's desire for revenge.

Sigrid (the Haughty): Swedish queen, mother of *Olaf Skotkonung*, widow of Erik the Victorious. Insulted *Olaf T.* during marriage negotiations and was struck by him and insulted in return. Later married *Sven Forkbeard*, making alliance between Sweden and Denmark against *Olaf T.*

Thyre: sister of *Sven F.*, married (i) *Styrbjorn*, viking cousin of Erik the V. of Sweden, (ii) *Boleslas* king of Vendland (Poland), (iii) *Olaf T.* whom she is reputed to have goaded into an unwise expedition to Vendland to claim properties settled on her second marriage.

Sigvaldi: Earl of Jomsborg and leader of the 'Jomsvikings', reputed to be crafty and untrustworthy. When the Jomsvikings attacked Norway in Haakon's reign, he fled from the battle of Jorundfjord, earning the 'scabby dog' epithet. Married to sister of *Boleslas*.

Naval battles were not uncommon at the time; an outnumbered fleet would lash ships together so that it could only be attacked easily over the outer gunwales, thus reducing the area of combat. At Svold this was overcome by Erik's ramming technique, sinking the outer ships and forcing them to be cut loose. Olaf's *Long Snake* was supposed to be the largest ship in the world, built to twice the dimensions of his former flagship *Snake*.

The lines from Bjornson's poem mean: 'Where is the *Long Snake*?/ Has Olaf Trygvason not come?'. The story of Olaf is told in Snorri Sturlusson's *Heimskringla* (c 1250).

NAVIGATOR

Into the deep dream
pale sails wind-gripped
I have trailed the wastes of sleep
the unmarked ocean march-strakes
the chartless waterways of night...

...where I have sighted islands
lost since every morning
ground on sandbars
humping underneath the hull
walked bleach-white beaches
and lain at evening
couched in hollow grasses
past the reaches of the sea...

...listening to music on the wind
ancient aeolian airs
tasting their quinine upon my tongue
grinding crystal salt between my teeth
taking pleasure in their citric sting...

...and in these infinitely far havens
felt longings ease
and peace envelop everything
like evening sun
warming still the distant waves
soaking pain from limbs
wrenched muscles
blistered skin...

...there I have met with friends long dead
spoken with surprise
that they should greet me
joked on their appearance of health
wondered why I ever should have
mourned or missed them...

...and I have visited old homes
places skeletal in memory
houses half forgotten
attics full of dust and broken toys
windows offering perspectives
formerly unseen...

...and though on these dream islands
I have encountered sorrows, too
seen devastated futures
children dead
or met (so many times)
the lost and unknown love
yet facing each return
to harbour in the grim dawn
I would go back
find the keel track in the waves
follow the furrow of the plunging stem.

+ + +

But I am a navigator
forced to draw on moth-wings
paper tenuous as early daylight
shellac-thin glass
that shatters at a touch...

...such charts as can be saved
on fragile, glittering mica-shards
I offer you.

AIR MOVING

Air moving in among the landscape features,
wind flowing, timeless river, moving air
over this undistinguished rise breaks into turbulence -
sea waves over islet white, and moving...

...while father, you, remembered, white, unmoving,
still as earth, as chalk-bone soil
to which you now return, for you
no flow of life, no moving air.

The land itself, the hollows and the levels,
fed, fertiled and disturbed by moving air,
feels it creep like water on its surface,
gently changing as the tidal air demands.

What calcined skeleton beneath supports
upholster soil and fibrous roots of grass and trees,
how constant is the profile of this curving country,
that knot of trees, of sorts, how long has stood?

And in this morning moving into midday
time measured, measuring the grain of air,
house living over by the spinney
where shelter, water, growing land ensured
human companionship for plants and soil
down years where air moved measureless, measuring...
air moving.

It would not do to die today,
would not be meet to separate
the flesh and pilot animus
in such a spell of early sun
of crocus daubs on sudden green
a season more for flight of new-fletched birds
in the fast grass-growth of the urchin year.

Beyond the curtained window
children playing in the early air of summer
can't envisage, as it were, a bridge
connecting spring with autumn;
each pillar needed for support
completing the existence of the other.
So each birth prophesied your death,
each grandchild marked a countdown to this morning.

And on a morning of such gently-moving air,
a lorry central to its ball of sound,
a never-bursting bubble stretched shapeless by the wind,
provides a pedal-tone on which the world can rest,
construct its harmonies upon a fundamental bass.

The moving air foretells so many things:
this coming truck-bassoon, the tunnel train,
the unknown storm, the anticyclone clear,
the rain, the sea-fog, the migrating birds;
and underneath the partly-plated sky
from all far places out across the world
brings dusts and smells and tastes of outland parts
as surely as its now slow moving in your chest and throat
marks out the imminence of your death.

That last slow raven-cry -
the spirit tearing up its roots?
Or just the failing breath,
the final slug of moving air
forced out past the collapsing tongue?

And who dares use the phrase 'democracy of death'?
This is no democrat that comes, inexorable,
crushing like an empty tube your withered husk.
Watching, I am crushed, and changed-about,
passing, as you pass, the final reach of boyhood.
And, father, have you also reached a childhood's-end?
Is there a place for you to go
the way our shared religion teaches?

I wish I could have thought
I felt your spirit leaving on its flight
borne into the birdsong of this moving air,
but what I saw was like a factory shutting down,
the switches pulled, lights going out,
windows darkened one by one,
watched consciousness evaporate as spirits will,
and all your knowledge, like a tape, erased.

This stilling of the air tests faith,
for when the passing-on is done
the body grounded finally
the relatives returned to anonymity,
even believers wonder why there is no sign,
no contact with the now-beloved dead.

Here on this rise, this other morning,
a lark displays itself between the sky and earth,
struggles, so it seems, to keep its hold on air.
How unbelievable its strength,
how rapidly would my arms become exhausted
had I to fight for height, to push aside the moving air...
yet that small body has the strength to spare to sing!

So, could it be, the newly-dead
wakening to unconceived dimensions
unable both to hold a place and sing
yet forced by birth to glorify the day
cannot help but lose their track
find their frame of reference disappeared
gone past rediscovery, past recall,
and matter not if wills, or whether wants, or wish,
but *cannot*, in such vastness, see such small?

As singing in the moving air
a voice; magnetic echo
down the ether tremulant,
voice of dead Caruso
living in the moving air,
or orchestras or choirs long disbanded,
organs muted, within whose tubes the air not-moves,
now like the lark, the soul, revital
through the engineer's control
of air and of its movement.

And other voices, millions, like in-transit spirits
haunting and competing for a second's speech,
peeping and squealing like a plague of bats,
yet with a metal line I trawl this live and moving air
selecting from the immolating shoal
one fish, one bat, one voice,
as coil commands the others go.

What stills the voice? When air is still.
His voice, once call-commanding
now, like airless organ-pipe, is mute;
like untuned air-voice sweeps away
to other, place-unknown receivers.

Warm water cannot help his cooling hands,
nor widow's tears relax his rigid face
and I, in eggshell-broken glass of promises
think what right I have to weep my father's death
with others' fathers dying by the minute.

If I were ordered now '*Pay what thou owest*!'
how would I make return on all my debt?
What value is a life, what worth has wisdom?
How much the service-charge, the interest?
And, father, I would pay you now in years
from off my life, breath given from my lungs;
yet all I do is place a tribute on your eyes,
two coins - grey moons reflecting back my selfish face -
and draw the sheet across them, cancelling
this final notice of my obligation.

Here on this morning rise I lie
observe the airflow measure time
cloud-bars skim the sky like clock-hands
bringing time across the moving air,
look for other places mirrored -
under that cloud lies Damascus
and under that, Tashkent,
and this, New York, that other, Lima,
those icy crystals there, the Pole,
and yet another punctured by the spire of Everest.

Sun moves across my foot
dispenses, with its inches, time,
marks my journey to the future cold,
slides me further from my history,
makes me more an exile with each inch:
we wander time like gypsies
unable ever to revisit or resettle in
whatever part we think about as home.

For time kills everything that lives,
and as I look at last at you it killed,
I know why saints are made of marble
glowing with an in-reflected light.
Within your satin cloths I watch your face
and see as if in mirrors
all the faces that you wore the long way back to childhood:
my face too is there -
only now I see how similar we were,
while you lived I thought we were so different,

In these considerations I put things in balance
taking succour from this place's permanence,
from wind, from weather-engine moving air,
from all far lands, from hanging lark,
from trees, from earth, from sound, from heat,
and you, your life, your death, your life-in-me,
and from the all-connecting air
in which birds swim and insects float,
which measures time, moves heat, makes sound,
and carries life...

... for, even now, through soil-chinks, gases creep,
oxygen, nitrogen:

air, moving...

FOLLOWING SPRINGTIME

(1985 - 1988)

1 FORTRESS FORTY

When you are young
when you are old enough
to realise your freedom
is just the chance to be a target
for the artillery of insult
with which life is so well equipped,
when you pick up a shield,
lay out a picket,
in your solicitude for safety
choose solitude,
it starts...

At twenty you begin to build
a wall of years, not thinking
that by thirty it will still be incomplete:
by then you'll need a parapet, a moat,
shutters, drawbridge, guards, alarms,
all the armoury of protection...

You're happy, building,
feeling safer by the day;
security, you say,
brings true contentment. And so
you seal the cracks, shoot bolts,
build coping stones on castellations,
until you find yourself ensconced
in Fortress Forty...

Within its fastness
you stay, ignorant of how
assurance has become incarceration,
locked in self-inflicted darkness,
you pace, puzzled,
waiting...

2 GIRL, OH GIRL

Girl, oh girl,
in darkness I await your light,
loiter for a word's
reward, meet you in the past and future
filigree of dreams, fall forever through the golden
galaxies of your eyes.

But time roars like a river,
rushing us apart. I stare across at you,
years adrift. I am aware
too well, of all that isolates.

Helpless, I interpret
interest from your body's semaphore,
synthesise from the grammar of your glance
grotesquely exaggerated expectations,
excruciatingly aware of what a fool
I feel, hoping out of hopelessness

although I know
those same athletic youths I fear,
feel so inadequate beside, are not
your need. All those callow
fellows, pass-artists, jab-johnnies who come
and go, are callously unaware:
I care.

Yet, fearing to lose the petty
privilege I own
over some unwanted move,
my courage collapses, saving
shame of rejection. Saving, too, the deeper
disillusion which awaits the one who, following
the springtime northwards, finds
it ends in unremitting winter.

3 LINES

These dozen dozing people hustled north
know nothing; outside, the inexorable night
like a black river pours past the window,
while I sit undistinguished
in this conventional seat,
sick with the ache of our first, last,
lost kiss...

in which we briefly touched
tongues, glued tender parts together,
tearing them too soon apart, leaving
lesions unhealed, fresh wounds bleeding questions...

Are you now feeling
relief? Pleased he's gone?
Glad it's over? Or
are you, too, raw, hurt
with regret?

Between the lines
of your letters, I cannot infer
your feelings. These steel lines
leading us apart
draw parallels...

We travel, like trains,
tracks from which there's no escape
except to chaos. Lifelines
lead to different
destinations, leave us
desolate on platforms, waving,
waving...

4 SHROVE TUESDAY

We meet again upon a needle-tip
of time, of hours metered down, you appearing
pristine -- dressed to kill, I feel,
fearing the immediate future, talking
trivia, asking twice about your health, job,
jokes, friends, earthquakes, anything...

Then you reach across the table, over
the river, take my hands, so that once again I fall
forever through your eyes, hear you somewhere
speak of love...

Later, in the cold streets, we kiss
careless as children tasting first
fruit. Feeling your tremor
I take your hand beneath my coat, my warmth
rewarded doubly as you smile,
striking out of darkness, light, making
from late winter,
spring.

5 NO FOOL

no fool, they say, he's
nobody's fool; made a new
career out of failure as an
engineer; writes, plays music, sings,
dabbles with a dozen tongues...

but they who say don't know, don't
see him seek the morning mail,
search anxiously for word of her,
nor did they see him wait each
evening, until her car had gone...

they cannot count the flutters
of his fatty heart when
he is waiting for her, nor
know how he is counting time
till they can meet again...

and when they say love's blind, they
cannot see, themselves, that love
in middle age is not so blind as just
unused, stepping like Lazarus, timid,
stiff, blinking, bound in cloths and cobwebs...

and age, they say, brings certitude, but
they couldn't be more wrong, because
it beings its fears, too: experience numbs,
for he has loved before, and failed,
and fear of repetition undermines...

fears are all around: death, decline, short
days, autumn; and, across the afternoon
the time-flower drops its petals, one by one, be-
tokening *she loves me, she* -- but,
as they have also said, there's no fool...

6 FOOL'S SONNET

Your eyes are oceans into which I fall
forever, pools where I'm content to drown.
Your mouth's the spring to which my lips are drawn
to drink, my tongue to taste, my wells refill.
My fingers know how soft your breasts would feel,
they ache for the experience of your skin.
In gambling for your smile, I'd risk your scorn;
for mere affection be your willing fool.

Yet even such a fool as I might be
can't sacrifice *all* pride for mere affection:
I clown for you, but always hope thereby
to lower your defences by a fraction --
enough, at least, to let your love deploy
from pity for your cunning fool's affliction.

7 DISTANCE

Distance does not lend
a thing! Its charge
is high, its interest
attenuated in a long
catenary, sagging like gum:
the further
the weaker.
        Enchantment is only
        when you are near, when
        with a touch, a signal
        flashed across from eyes,
        love flickers
        into fragile life.
Absence breaks the heart
asunder. Do you get
the pun, dear? The
bitter joke? Apart,
the river drowns sound,
stifles, stultifies.
Wounds remain unbound,
lines meet
only at infinity.

8 NOW THAT YOU'RE GONE

Is last love
love that lasts,
or is it indecisive, querulous,
crippled with prior wounds,
fears, fantasies...?

> Now that you've gone,
> I move like one who limps
> to ease familiar pain, favouring
> arthritis, repeating:
> I can survive; no-one
> ever died of love.

You say you do not love;
I say you lie,
lie to save yourself pursuit
of something lost, but
most of all, lie
to save my seeking
unattainable spring.
In such a lie
you prove your love.

> I would have had you think me god --
> I think you thought me father,
> a father-god creating what
> he thought was you around
> his own thought-image, as far
> from what you think you are
> as what you think I am.

And I? I have pursued you decorously,
too decorously, perhaps. Waiting for signals,
I should have seized, yet,
when I tried, your fingers slipped away.
I watched you vanish down the line
down the river, drawn
by season and by time.

> Now that you're gone, I know
> I snatched at spring
> only to feel it shatter in my hands
> like the last sheer ice of winter.

PLACES OF WORK

(1980 - 92)

JETTY: JANUARY

Outside, the cold is stunning, shocking;
boots, jerseys, wintersocks, boilersuits
are poor protection;
this wind was born in Spitzbergen
has experience of Eskimos, Norwegians, Poles,
it finds my thin meat easy,
picks my English bones...

We want them covers off
Can't sit in here all day
The filters is half-blocked
With shit already.

The river is a slab of slime
the colour of slugs,
too thick with grease to freeze;
the sky is resting on the chimneys
spreading solid smoke
as thin, grey snow...

Forty-two nuts each cover plate
Slack them off with a hammer first
Here, use this spanner, lad. Then give's a shout
I'll do the rest.

In the raw air
finger-joints don't work,
swell, chap, redden in the wet cold;
eyes, nose, flood;
metal sucks heat, cuts painlessly deep...

Remember, lad, a tap
Will never loosen them -
They're rusted up,
And clouting them'll keep you warm!

I belt the battered spanner-steel
unwilling nuts creak, give, turn,
I miss, strike a naked knuckle,
do not notice blood
viscous on my filthy skin.

I only see the spanner fall,
clank, ricochet from angle-iron
into the waiting water...
You clumsy sod!
You stupid berk!
Don't send a lad
On man's work!

I don't know which is worst,
the shame
of failing in this male regime,
the pain
returning to my battered hand,
or knowing, here in the warm,
I have to go outside again.

FIRST LOVES: FEBRUARY

I loved them hopelessly
knowing they would go...
One, I met in secret
for her parents' sake
she on her way to Mass, and I to work;
a desperate kiss, a brief embrace
before we had to separate.
Black Candlemas...
The other waited wantonly
behind the fitting shop
sharp breast ellipse
outlined against the winter dawn:
cool nordic beauty:
Bergensfjord...
The girl from grammar school
is long gone now, moved away,
married, middle-aged,
like me, grey,
and *Bergensfjord*'s a rusting wreck,
or sails below some lesser flag,
renamed, past recognition.
...Hopelessly I record, before they go,
beloved, fading images.

OPERA: BOILER TOPS

Lapping valves: carborundum eroding steel.
In the dark ravine between the boiler tops
we crouch in noise and heat, the beat
of massive engines, and their oil-sweet breath...
Like bushmen making fire
we huddle, spin the stick
between hardened palms
the lapping tool abrading, abrading
the hours until we eat
or drink, or shit
or otherwise escape from here...
Not as much paste!
You're wastin' it
We'll need to go for more
afore we're done
Spud, the fitter
jittery at his unskilled apprentice
I, stammering, embarrassed
(*sorry, Spud*) and polish, polish...
Keep it flat, lad, look
you've made a mark!
It'll take another hour
to get that out...
I apologise again, despair
of ever being an engineer
recognise the tune he whistles
lift my head, still polishing, sing...
O dolci bacio
O languide carezze
Mentr'io fremente
*Le belle forme discoglea dai veli...**
He is amazed (*Where'd you larn to sing like that?*)
Me too: a fitter whistling Tosca (*Didn't know you liked that sort of thing*)
He spreads the word, my fame (*Hey, lads, have ye heard this kid* ***sing****?*)

...and we are at the opening
of apposite companionship
of concerts on the boiler tops
comparisons with Caruso, Lanza, Björling
foremen looking puzzled, labourers
lapping up opera.

* *from 'E Lucevan le Stelle', Tosca, Puccini/Illica*

WIND TUNNEL: JULY

Mach two-point-two:
the tunnel shrieks
unbelievably, ear-bleedingly loud:
one-three-two deebee...

Noise insulates, isolates
more effectively than silence;
wool-stuffed, phone-muffed ears,
speakers, mikes, swamped,
we communicate like mutes,
signing...

Sheer sound exhausts,
lies like a load upon the air,
sickening resonances in the thorax,
feet shaking in the shoes...

We adjust manometers, protractors,
scribble figures into boxes
on report sheets,
wave to one another, change the settings,
readjust, read again...

We, the undeaf, incommunicado,
hallucinate. Strange memories
surface, things unthought, dark scenes
seen fleetingly in half-sleep
come, conscious, to us now...

Wind-tunnel, time-tunnel:
as with the action of a drug,
noise, warmth and boredom dull the brain,
make the mind escape
down pathways to the past,
the future, other places.

Out of the noise-mist
poems emerge...

LUNCH-HOUR: AUGUST

Sun transforms the land:
railtracks gleam,
steelbright solid lines of light
set in the hot dust
musty with coal and oil...

boilersuit-stripped
the lads lounge
billycans, baitboxes,
sandwiches, smokes

In the distance, the river
glitters like molten tar,
starved of rain,
its sewer-taint reaches us...

talk of holidays,
caravans up the coast:
Spain had not yet
set its chips and bingo trap

Summer has come to the shipyards:
half-built hulls hide rabbits,
skulking cats too hot to hunt;
truce breaks out in football, politics, all
too well aware how rare
this warmth is
in the north...

ignore the buzzers, stay
dozing for another minute
eyelid-inners
orange with sun

Concrete, iron
briefly lose their grip:
on the sidings, bankings,
in the cracks, between the sleepers,
fireweed, wickens
proliferate.

JACK: ACCIDENT REPORT

Home soon son -- you sick?
Sick! I cannot speak for shock

Investigations indicate
several causative fact-
ors: first, incorrect
slinging of the bedplate...

It's a sort of half-day strike
we've been sent home from work

non-standard slings, which had not
been properly maintained
were used beyond safe working load
with hooks instead of shackle-bolts...

There was an ac-
cident: a crane-hook broke

before the lift was complete
the crane traversed;
as a result, the load
fouled a handrail, and a tilt...

a bloke, a helpless little bloke
was killed -- we used to talk

open hooks thus came out
of the eyebolts, and the load
slipped; the slings snapped
the bedplate fell twenty feet...

Jack: scrubby hair, quick eyes, just like
a little mole, a whistling lark:
crushed meat, extruded lungs, crack-
ed ribs spread on the deck.
Even the first-aid-man was sick.

NOTICE IS HEREBY GIVEN THAT
UNCERTIFIED SLINGS MUST BE DESTROYED
THAT ONLY BOLTED SHACKLES MAY BE USED
THAT STAFF STAND CLEAR WHEN LIFTING LOADS

Will you look
at that, they said, makes you think,
eh, how they always lock
the door after the fuck-
ing horse has gone. But I was stuck
with Jack, little Jack
gone too, flat as a bug
beneath a boot, as a dog
beneath a truck.

LAUNCH: SEPTEMBER

The ship goes to the water,
the gaffers to their whisky,
the workers to the wall
and the dole.

So says convention. But
have those who quote it
heard those same lads cheer their ship
as she eases down the slip?

MAN AND BOY: DISC TEST HOUSE

Fitting up the next disc, he sang...
Awa' i' th' Northland
There leeved a wee lassie,
Wha skint a' her knee
On a wee chucky stane...
...we laughed, not knowing how he'd fall,
Jock the fitter, dead as a sack
before his head hit the deck
heart attack at 50, five months hence...
Come on, you Scotch git
get that bastard nipped up
before it's time to stop...
Ah, feck aff! Ye'll hae tae wait...
We were the men who measured metal-death
testing discs of steel in oil
working out the wear
of gear on gear, in miniature...
Ach, see wha's comin'
Yon wee cocky cunt!
We're for a dose o' bullshit noo.
Man, that's a' we need!
New from college, corners still intact,
insensitive to how much he was disliked
Ha, we'll be a'reet, son.
noo ye've come tae honour us.
Whit wisdom hae ye fer us
this efternuin?
Jock nipped the final nut another inch,
The bumptious bugger leaned against a bench,
behind him, Number Two Disc suddenly cracked
and he was off and running...
Well Ah'll be fecked!
Ah'd be"er shut that bogger doon
afore Ah piss masel' wi' fright
Jock stripped the damaged disc, and sang...
An' noo that wee lassie's
The Whoor o' Dunblane!

Poor dead Jock, toughness overwhelmed.
Poor frightened boy, shouting in the wind.

WORK BUS: NOVEMBER

Green steel haven
after the cold queue
in the morning storm;
we rush the upper deck
greedy for smoke
in the charcoal dawn.

Choir of coughs:
tenor, bass, terminal;
green steel coffin, of
rattling rivets, chests,
ceiling brown with slime
sliding down wet glass.

Today, for certain, we will
work with mercury, lead,
wash with trichloroethylene,
wipe down with carbon tet,
breathe asbestos-hairs,
and nicotine, nicotine,
never knowing, never noticing
the small intrusions,
the imperceptible symptoms.

Years from now,
they'll trace the sources
of our coronaries and cancers,
but we will never recollect
the rattling steel green
coughing coffin-haven,
nor ask for its inclusion
in the factors
we are taught to blame.

LATE TRAVELS

(1993 - 1996)

ALMOST A DROWNING

It is one of those Mediterranean days
at a place with a holiday name
and the sun slamming down so big
there is nowhere to be
but the sea.

And it looks so safe, so kind,
all those kids and old folks
splashing in the waves
begging you to come,
have fun.

We do, we do. It's just so hot, so dry,
although I'm able to swim
only a stroke or two
salt water's fine
it supports you.

Suddenly it doesn't:
toes scrabble sand scouring
in the undertow, waves smash down,
the shore is further than the sun
shouts fail among the fun

I swim with all the strength I have
to no avail; all
I can see of the shore
is further than before
around me only waves and noise.

Of course, my friend brings help, arms pull me back,
I stumble in the shallows, spent and blowing.
Now, sea-reborn, I think I know
what life is worth
and where I'm going.

AUVERGNE AUTUMN

The Xhosa has a score of words for *green*,
the Inuit a dozen or so for *snow*,
each distinguishes the relevant
where *wet-green* equals life and *dry-green* death,
or *crisp-snow* gets you home while *soft-top* kills.

Today I want to find a set of words for *gold*
to call the colours of the forest slopes,
I need, like Japanese, to have a word
for *pale-hills-in-the-morning-mist*,
or *purple-mountains-at-the-door-of-night.*

I want to find a set of words for *age*,
for, though its rays still saturate my skin
and fool the butterflies into thinking it's still June,
there's nothing crueller than October sun --
that same grim month that claims me for another year.

And most of all I need a set of words for *love*,
for *love-that's-dead*, for *love-that-never-was*
(or *-never-could-be*), *love-that-might-have-been*,
or *love-to-come.* God! *Love-to-come*!
Is that word in whatever glossary remains?

PUB DOG

(*Le Murrayfield Scottish Pub, Bourges, France*)

The pub dog,
dark and shaggy old rug
head and tail bowed, deaf,
a dog-year octogenarian,
wanders among the feet
survives, uncomplaining, the accidental kick,
lifts sad, blind eyes to a touch.

Only his nose twitches
painting the strange scent-pictures
he's known throughout his life
in patterns we cannot imagine
persisting through time as sound and light do not;
he knows more than we do
in ways we cannot understand.

Though you may want to
do not pity him.
All he has lost
are the distractions:
light, sound, anger, sex.
Brain and smell and images remain
clear as in his young-dog days.

TANK BATTLE

In the tank, the *langoustes* fight
struggle with bound claws to pierce armour
fruitlessly engage in internecine war.

In Bosnia, the tanks are struggling again
fighting as pointlessly as the carapaced crustacea
corralled within their tank with death the only out.

Have you seen the sheer destruction of a tank battle,
that Sinai graveyard, strewn with tons
of burned bodies, melted metal, bound with miles of missile-wire?

Then think what it was like at Kursk,
when ten thousand motorised panthers
clashed from east and west and Left and Right.

Do you realise what a ballet there has been
between the tank and the projectile, first the one
then the other gaining the advantage?

And have you seen what shaped-charge rounds
can do to heavy armour, blasting it to blowtorch fragments
shredding any crew within?

So, of course, you think it's sad
how human ingenuity has worked so hard
at learning how to kill

how modern shells spray poison, fire,
showers of tiny bombs, each smaller than a soup-can
capable of chopping infantry or killing tanks.

Yes, from Cambrai to Alamein,
Kursk to Korea, Cambodia,
from the Tigris to the Sava, the tanks have struggled,

as, in the tank, the *crevettes* struggle,
pointlessly, not knowing they must die. And though *we* do,
still we fight: yes, take away our tanks, we'd fight with sticks.

PRAGUE 1970

Pan Novák, dobrý den
I'm glad that it's all over now
and we are free again.

Pan Pluskal, dá-li bůh
with '45 behind us too
we're very liberated men!

Liberation, *příteli,*
what is this, do you think?

A different uniform, my friend,
a different make of tank!

BARCELONA 1985

Viva Catalunya Lliure
cries yesterday's graffito.
But in the luminous alleys
of the *Barrio Gotico*, voices squabble
in cobbled Catalan, and in the cathedral
Sant Maria, Mar de Deu is whispered
while red-and-gold
decorates the *Generalitat.*
Then in the *Plaça del San Felip*, you understand:
the shattered stone where automatic fire
bled yesterday's martyrs.

BELGRADE 1990

Where
the Sava meets the Dunai
we dined, none thinking there'd be
war.

Yet
the taxidriver let it fall:
bastard dirty Muslim, we should make all
shot!

LAST NIGHT

Last night in France, heading for Calais,
Arras, names of battles,
Béthune, Cambrai...

Low clouds crush the land
against the vampire chalk, pale,
thirsting for more young blood.

Last night out:
a Greek restaurant appeals,
mock temple crossing Parthenon with Crete,

and I see the Knossos woman
realise that someone four millennia dead
is pictured on this wall.

But when the young *maître d'*
chats in French about Iraklion and Elounda,
a shock of recognition:

the oval eyes, the snaking curls
the pale skin, the turned up mouth,
that woman is his mother, many times removed!

Then, over coffee, thinking of the young dead
for whom this place became their
last night in France, or anywhere,

and wondering, four thousand years from now,
who will see their faces,
recognise their eyes, their hair?

ROCHELLE

(for Steve)

She guarded the approaches from the south and west
north of Bordeaux, south of St Nazaire
the fortress harbour at the waist of France.

But now two hundred sailing craft
bring the banners of the world to La Rochelle
and tourists throng her restaurants.

We, tourists, sitting on the quayside
savouring the sea-bass and the wine
ordering another bottle,

laughing, telling jokes,
talking of the women in our lives, music, poetry,
sharing friendship-building confidences...

Only the cold wind at my back hinted
how summer was sailing from the harbour
south and west.

FIRE AND WATER

(Fountain: Arles)

The physics of the fountain flickers
at the edge of comprehension:

its central pillar quivers like cold fire
surrounded by a crystal crown of water,

varies with its pressures, balanced
like blown curtains on a summer wind

or like the *parapentes* that soar
around the Puy de Dôme.

Their impacts interacting with the central column
engender random changes as they fall,

and, as gas escapes from coal,
grasping oxygen in shifting tones of heat,

this water gives its substance to the air
spreading the deep earth's welcome cold in summer,

but, now, its damp chill spreads even to my room
makes me write of autumn, and of coming death.

AUTUMN SMOKE

(1975)

Diesel fume and chimney gas
screen the city
dusk October,
gardeners reduce to ash
the petty
corpse of summer:
I wish I could afford
abroad, instead
of visiting my mother.

I would recall the foreign talk
the coins
reflecting warmer sun,
Pernod, perhaps, or armagnac,
or wines
beneath a parasol;
but I have just
the dust, the Tyne,
and Amber Ale.

No, the smoke that really smarts
my eyes
is not the dark
device
of diesel or of furnace,
not wreaths from throwaway
old flowers, but
Gauloises, gifts
recalling someone else's holiday.

ANCIENT STONES

Over the flat lands of France
thin roads ruled straight
across the map, strung
with speed-limited villages,
trees, farms, few vehicles
or other signs of life:
suddenly, out of the haze
the hulking mass of Chartres,
man's pile of ancient stones
placating the gods.

Later, further down the long roads
across the slashes of the Loire and Rhone,
the low, vine-furred hills,
I discover, rising in the distance
the unbelievable wall of the Alps:
the gods' response in stone.

LUNCH IN VADUZ

Atlas-poring, twelve years old, I found Vaduz
a crisp, romantic name, all v's and z's,
and tiny Liechtenstein
tight-packed with mystery.

Years later, driving Europe
I lunched there, in an English pub,
on English ale and omelette...
tasting only bitterness.

WARMING

May should never be so warm
the growers claim
and pray for rain...

...but where I lie
the sky is such a virgin-blue
traverse for birds, while early flies
negotiate the lower air
I controvert their prayer...

...perhaps I've reached the stage
where age determines how I act
where bones reach out for warmth
reject the rheumatising chill
with which our weather-driven
work-ethic compels us...

...for once we have a taste of south
of lazy days in which tomorrow
may mean soon
or may mean not at all...

...and all the flowers and the birds
who watch uncomprehending
how we labour for so long
achieve so little, die so soon
agree with me, and harmonise
the river's incantation...

...grass and leaves and water know the score
chance is we may never know such summer more
adore the sun...

SPRING, YOU BITCH

Spring, you bitch, with your Easter face,
presenting eggs of resurrection,
virgin snowdrops, crocus pricks.

You make Good Friday bloom in thorns
with all the pain of birth
commemorating death,

let low skies crack and slough
to show a pale high blue presaging summer
and the blessings of the sacred sun,

mould cumuli of blossom on the naked branch
slap daubs of gold and purple onto every green
smash them flat in gales to suit your humour's change.

You looked upon my parents' deaths
laughing as we sowed their flesh in April clay
in the month of their birth.

You stimulate the blood,
seduce us with illusions of our youth,
making us forget the doom that lurks in every growing cell,

deceiving us with each bright morning, each new leaf,
you graceful careless child, dancing beyond our reach,
Spring, you bitch, you bitch, you lovely, lying bitch!

WINTER CAMPAIGN

On the last day of October, by the Middle Sea
watching her cast her troops against the shore
waves of indefatigible infantry,
thinking how she gave me back my life
casting me back from near-drowning...

winter is moving divisions out of the north
capturing Scandinavia and Scotland,
parachuting snow-battalions into the high Alps,
shutting down forests which glow briefly
with the colours of fading heat
before they die...

I travelled south, seeking to escape his depredations,
sat above the Loire, looking to the warmth of
red wine in the dying year,
saw in Orange, city the colour of autumn,
ancient ruins golden in the afternoon,
and Avignon, with its broken bridge
chilly in the winds above the Rhone.

In Arles, its obelisk a needle to the rose-lit sky,
its circular fountain a frigid flame,
I lay in a cold hotel room, writing poems
fighting the chill, feeling yet another autumn birthday
move off into the night...

but, even here, a year older than yesterday,
warm in southern sun,
feel winter silently encircling me,
and ask *Old Lady Sea of Middle Earth,*
is there a reason that you gave me back my life,
or, like the patterns in the fountain,
was it simply random,
interesting, but quite devoid of meaning?